AUTHORS OF THE MIDDLE AGES

English Writers of the Late Middle Ages

Sir John Mandeville

M.C. Seymour

Variorum

AUTHORS OF THE MIDDLE AGES . 1
English Writers of the Late Middle Ages: General Editor, M.C. Seymour

Published by   VARIORUM
Ashgate Publishing Limited
Gower House, Croft Road
Aldershot, Hants GU11 3HR
UK

Ashgate Publishing Company
Old Post Road
Brookfield, Vermont 05036
USA

A CIP catalogue record for this book is available from the British Library.

ISBN 0–86078–371–5

Typeset by   Manton Typesetters,
7 Eastfield Road, Louth,
Lincolnshire LN11 7AJ

Printed and Bound in Great Britain by
Athenaeum Press Ltd, Newcastle upon Tyne.

CONTENTS

SIR JOHN MANDEVILLE

PART I. The Facts

PART II. The Fictions

BIBLIOGRAPHY

ABBREVIATIONS

AnM	Analecta Medievalia
AUMLA	Australian University Modern Language Association
BL	British Library, London
BN	Bibliothèque Nationale, Paris
ES	English Studies
MLN	Modern Language Notes
MLQ	Modern Language Quarterly
MLR	Modern Language Review
MP	Modern Philology
NM	Neuphilologische Mitteilungen
NQ	Notes & Queries
PMLA	Publications of the Modern Language Association of America
RES	Review of English Studies

SIR JOHN MANDEVILLE
PART I. THE FACTS

The nature of the inquiry

When *Mandeville's Travels* appeared *c.* 1357 its author claimed to be Sir John Mandeville, an English knight, born and bred in St Albans, who had left England in 1322 and travelled the world for thirty-five years, finally writing his account from memory in his old age. For two hundred years, when copies of the book in manuscripts and early prints circulated throughout Europe, this claim was universally accepted. Even after 1550, when the more fabulous parts of the book began to bring the whole into disrepute in the eyes of some, Sir John Mandeville never lacked sturdy supporters. For example, in the eighteenth century at roughly the same time that an anonymous reader wrote in his copy of an early English edition

> No occasion to Travel, to write such stuff. A Fool with a wimsical head furniture may do it at Home,[1]

Steele wrote in *The Tatler* 22 November 1710 'our renowned Countryman *Sir John Mandeville* has distinguished himself by the Copiousness of his Invention, and Greatness of his Genius', and was followed by Dr. Johnson in the preface to his Dictionary in 1755 who praised the work for its 'force of thought and beauty of expression'.

This see-saw reputation, more commonly up than down, surrounded the book until the late nineteenth century when investigations into other contemporary and near-contemporary travel books of the thirteenth and fourteenth centuries showed, beyond question for the most part, that the author had in fact 'done it at Home'.[2] Yet even in the midst of this detailed cataloguing of the books from which *Mandeville's Travels* had been compiled, scholarly caution prompted a *caveat*:

> Nor does it follow that the whole work is borrowed or fictitious...in Mandeville also we find particulars not yet traced to other writers and which

In the footnotes citations by name are to entries in the bibliography of Secondary Sources. Citations of French and English editions of *Mandevilles Travels* by editor and short title are to works listed in the bibliography of Editions.

1 De Worde, 1503 edition fol. cii^v, in the Bodleian Library, Douce frag. e. 8.

2 Bovenschen in 1888 and G.F. Warner ed., *The Buke of John Maundeuill* (1889), working independently.

may therefore be provisionally assigned either to the writer's own experience or to knowledge acquired by colloquial intercourse in the East.[3]

These findings and this *caveat* caused the see-saw of reputation to swing more violently, and the identity of the author and so the nature of the book, in whole and in part, became in the twentieth century matters of debate involving everyone who as reader, editor, or scholar touched the work. For a time a physician, Jean de Bourgogne, alias Jean à la barbe, who died at Liège in 1372, was thought to be the author.[4] Then Jean d'Outremeuse, a Liège notary and chronicler (d. 1400), who was first responsible, it seems, for the association of Jean de Bourgogne with *Mandeville's Travels*, was himself credited with the work.[5] In 1949 the case for a genuine English knight, Sir John Mandeville, as the book claims, was put forward and re-stated in 1953.[6] In 1954 a similar argument, though on a different base, was made.[7] In 1963 a dissenting voice claimed that the author was a French-speaking cleric.[8] And in 1986, partly reflecting this view, the Oxford History of English Literature reported:

'Sir John Mandeville' is rather more fictitious than the work attributed to him, which is saying a good deal. There can hardly be any doubt that no such knight was ever dubbed or that the name is a pseudo-nym devised by the clever compiler of the book of the *Travels*.[9]

In 1988, however, the case for a genuine English Sir John Mandeville was again, with some qualifications, put forward.[10] Two opposing views are thus current: the first, maintained by English scholars, that the author was not an English knight; the second, now held mainly by Belgian scholars, that he was an Englishman who lived at Liège.

These various views of authorship are reflected in editions and literary histories of the twentieth century, though nowadays some writers report the conflicting theories without embracing one or the other and then comment on the work, a practice of dubious value since an understanding of its origins is crucial to an understanding of the book. Part of the problem has lain

3 Nicholson and Yule.
4 Warner, *op. cit.*, pp. xxx–xl.
5 P. Hamelius ed., *Mandeville's Travels* (1919), pp. 8–13.
6 Letts 1949, pp. 13–22 and in his edition (1953) I. xvii–xxiv argues that Bourgogne was the *alias* of Sir John Mandeville.
7 Bennett, *Rediscovery*, pp. 89–216 argues that the Insular Version is the primary text, written by Mandeville in England. She develops the idea, first set down in a review of Letts 1949, that the Liège connection with Mandeville is spurious.
8 M.C. Seymour, *The Bodley Version of Mandeville's Travels* (1963), p. 176.
9 J.A.W. Bennett, *Middle English Literature* (1986), p. 359.
10 Deluz pp. 363–4, who argues for a mature, well-read layman.

in the complex relationship of over 250 manuscripts in French, Latin, English, Czech, Danish, Dutch, German, Irish, and Spanish and in the absence of a critical, if not a definitive edition of the original French book. Thus, in 1921 one scholar felt confident enough to state of the English versions:

> It is unlikely that any simple formula will be found to cover the whole web of relationships.[11]

Fortunately this view proved unfounded. Since 1955 scholars in universities throughout Europe, enlightened by the basic research of the previous seventy years, have made clear much that was dark in the textual tradition, and it is now possible to construct a *stemma* which comprehends the affiliations of all versions and their sub-groups, with the important qualification that the relationship of the two primary French versions has still to be resolved exactly. Such a *stemma* shows indisputably the superiority of the French book, confirming the author's own statement that he wrote *en rommant*. Furthermore, since all other non-French versions of the work are demonstrably the redactions and translations of other men, they can, initially at least, be disregarded in the quest for the author. The French book alone provides whatever primary evidence exists for the identity of Sir John Mandeville.

The French versions

The French book, however, is not a simple text, for there are three French versions, each named after its provenance:

1. The Continental Version, extant in 31 manuscripts and mainly written in France. The earliest dated copy of this version was made in 1371 by the Parisian stationer Raoul d'Orléans for Gervaise Crétien, physician to Charles V. This copy contains numerous scribal corruptions and must lie at some remove from its lost archetype; it was originally associated with a French translation of Jean de Bourgogne's plague tract.[12] The early French prints, which appeared from 1480 to 1550, give this version.[13] It is distinguished by the presence of a long passage in the account of the Valley Perilous and a shorter passage in Chapter 20 concerning the climates of the world, neither of which are found in the Insular Version.[14]

11 Sisam p. 242.
12 Bibliothèque nationale fonds français nouv. acq. 4515, printed by Letts in his edition of 1953, and described by L. Delisle, *Catalogue des manuscrits des fonds Libri et Barrois* (1888), pp. 251–3. The plague tract was *compile a Liege...m.ccc.lxv.*
13 Bennett, *Rediscovery*, pp. 337–45 lists 13 editions between 1480 and 1550.
14 De Poerck 1956, pp. 135–40.

2. The Insular Version, extant in 23 manuscripts, appeared in England before 1390 when a copy of a Latin translation of it was written at Abingdon Abbey.[15] It is distinguished from the Continental Version by its dialectal colouring of Anglo-French forms and idioms, by some rephrasing, by the absence of part of the account of the Valley Perilous and by the presence in Chapter 20 of a paragraph concerning the climates of the world where the Continental Version has an alternative passage. This was the version of *Mandeville's Travels* known to and used by Chaucer and the poet of *Cleanness*.[16] A manuscript of this version was imported into France before 1402, while a manuscript of the Continental Version which had once belonged to Charles V (given to him by Gervaise Crétien) was obtained by Jean d'Angoulême in England during his captivity after Agincourt.[17]

3. The Liège Version, extant in 7 manuscripts, is a recension of the Continental Version. From internal references it may be located at Liège in or shortly after 1373. Its chief characteristics are the presence of several interpolations concerning Ogier le Danois, one of Charlemagne's legendary *douzpers*, who also features extensively in *Ly Myreur des Histors* of Jean d'Outremeuse, the Liège chronicler; the addition of two spurious alphabets of Cathay and the land of Prester John; and the interpolation in the epilogue of a reference to Jean de Bourgogne.[18]. The Liège Version is of primary importance in the development of the Mandeville myth that claims that *Mandeville's Travels* was written at Liège, but it is of no value in determining the authorship and provenance of the original work.

The relationship of the Continental and Insular Versions is unclear. One investigator, after a very cursory comparison of these two states of the French book, declared:

> the manuscripts written in England in Norman-French represent most faithfully the work of the author;[19]

---

15 Leiden, Bibliotheek der Rijksuniversiteit MS. Vulcan 96, written by Richard Bledelewe, monk of Abingdon, in 1390.

16 Cf. Brown, Bennett 1953, May who note some general correspondences without identifying the version used by Chaucer. The occurrence of the phrase *caue of Galilee* (a variant of the better *Chane in Galilee*) in *Wife of Bath's Prologue* line 11 suggests that Chaucer may have used the Insular Version where the corruption originates.

17 BN fonds fr. nouv. acq. 4515 (see note 1 above) was carried from France into England and back again: P. Champion, *La librairie de Charles d'Orléans* (1910), p. 71, n. 1. BN fonds fr. 5635 was written in France in 1402 from a copy made in England.

18 De Poerck 1961, pp. 31–2.

19 Bennett, *Rediscovery*, p. 146.

But this claim was immediately challenged by another who, after detailed collation of the major passages unique to each version, concluded that these textual discrepancies are complementary, and that both these French texts derive independently from the lost archetype.[20] The differences between the versions go far beyond these major passages, however,[21] and the reality of their relationship can only be determined by a critical edition of both texts, printed side by side with a full collation of all the extant copies of each. With other, dependent versions of the book it is often possible to pin-point exactly the subgroup of the anterior version from which the dependent derives, and no doubt in due course the relationship of the Continental and Insular Versions will be discovered with similar accuracy.

Fortunately for an investigator probing the problems of authorship, these textual complexities and uncertainties do not present an insuperable problem. The passages in both versions which throw light on the identity of the author differ only in minutiae which can be easily noted and accommodated in the argument. On present evidence it would appear that the Continental Version has the earlier and better text, and it is cited as *Mandeville's Travels* in the following pages from the copy dated 1371, with page references to the printed edition of 1953, which notes the more important differences between it and the Insular Version.

The date of composition

In the prologue the author states that he wrote in 1357:

> en recordant le temps passe iay ces choses copulees et mis en escript tout ainsi quil men puet souuenir lan de grace mil ccc. lvii. le xxxv^e. an que je me party de nostre pays. (p. 411)

Dates expressed in roman numerals were always liable to scribal confusion, and here the French manuscripts do show some variation; in general, though with variant readings in a few manuscripts of each tradition, the Continental Version records the date as 1357 and the Insular Version as 1356. There can be no certainty about the author's intention at this point. But whether he wrote 1357 or 1356, the actual date of composition was clearly *c.* 1357. The author based a large part of the second half of his book, which describes regions beyond the Holy Land, on the French translations of genuine Latin itineraries which Jean le Long (d. 1388), a Benedictine at the abbey church of St Bertin at St Omer (26 miles south-east of Calais) had completed in

20 De Poerck 1956, p. 136.
21 Letts in 1953 prints his collation of the Insular Version (as printed in Warner's edition of 1889) as an apparatus to his edition of the Continental Version.

1351, which is thus a *terminus a quo* for *Mandeville's Travels*.[22] Equally obviously, 1371 (the date of the copy made for Gervaise Crétien) is a *terminus ante quem*. When time is allowed for the copying and spreading afield of le Long's translations and for the development of the scribal tradition which produced the corruptions in the copy dated 1371, a date of composition *circa* 1357 cannot be very far from the truth. Initially the author must have been his own scribe, and the circumstances of its transcription by others after 1357 would have offered no incentive for fabrication and little scope for major error because the date of departure in the prologue is controlled by the date of composition and years spent *en voyage* in the epilogue. This dating *c.* 1357 receives some slight confirmation from an observation in the prologue,

> il a lonc temps que il ny ot passage general oultre mer.

Though a further offensive against the Saracens was no longer practical after the fall of Acre in 1291 and the subsequent collapse of the Kingdom of Jerusalem, the idea of a crusade was actively canvassed throughout the fourteenth century[23] and eventually resulted in the abortive expedition of Pierre de Lusignan against Alexandria in 1365. This reference in *Mandeville's Travels* to a *passage general* 'crusade' would thus appear to relate to a time before 1365.

There are some other vague temporal references in the French book which have seemed to some to offer evidence for an alternative dating. In Chapter 1 the author lists the possessions of the king of Hungary:

> il tient Hongrie, Sclauonie, et des Comains la plus grant partie, et Bulgarie que on appelle la terre des Bougres, et tient du royaume de Rousie grant partie, dont il a fait duche qui dure iusques a la terre de Niflan et marchist a Pruce, (p. 232)

which suggests the latter half of the reign of Louis the Great (1342–82) who conquered Bulgaria in 1365 and was crowned king of Poland in 1370.[24] But since these lands are already reported as part of the kingly style in 1347,[25] they may reflect more the royal pretensions, in a manner characteristic of medieval royal titles, than actual possessions.

---

22 This claim of dependence on Jean le Long is based on a comparison of the forms of exotic names but, in the absence of critical editions, is subject to caution.

23 A.S. Atiya, *Crusade in the later Middle Ages* (1938), p. 302, n. 3, citing a document of 1345. The *Directorium ad passagium*, one of the sources of 'Mandeville', is essentially an intelligence report for a crusade. See further K.M. Setton, *A history of the Crusades* II (2nd ed., 1969).

24 Warner ed., *op. cit.*, p. 197, n. 4 and Steiner.

25 Bennett, *Rediscovery*, p. 151, n. 8.

In Chapter 6 the author claims to have left Egypt during the caliphate of *Melechinam Damron* (p. 248) who, if his list of caliphs is chronologically accurate, may be identified as Malik al-Ashraf (1341–2). This reference is of no help in dating the work. Equally the statement in Chapter 10 that the Saracens have occupied the Holy Land

par lespace de vii. vins ans et xiiii (p. 268)

must derive from a written source of 1341, i.e. 154 years after the fall of Jerusalem in 1187; the Insular Version adds *et pluis*, which would appear to be a scribal updating; but neither reading helps date *Mandeville's Travels*.

In Chapter 24 the author records the proclamation of Chingis Khan 'universal khan', which occurred in 1206, as

il a plus de iiii. vins ans. (p. 355)

At this point the author follows Haiton, *La flor des estoires de la terre d'Orient*, written before 1308, who does not date the Khan's election. But Vincent of Beauvais, *Speculum historiale* XXIX. 69, another of the sources of *Mandeville's Travels*, gives the date as 1202. If one then believes that a variant reading *viii*^{xx} *ans* once existed (for which the only evidence occurs in the English translations) and was the author's reading, the reference may be dated 1362, i.e. 160 years after Vincent's date of 1202. This tenuous argument is wholly unconvincing.[26]

One subgroup of the Insular Version includes a Latin dedication to Edward III (1312–77), among whose titles it gives *Aquitanie Duci*.[27] Aquitaine was ceded to the English by the Treaty of Calais in 1360 but reverted to the French in 1375, when it was formally surrendered by the Truce of Bruges. Even if the dedication is contemporary and not posthumous and reflects reality and not pretension, there is no reason to regard it as an integral part of *Mandeville's Travels*. Another interpolation which seems to derive from the same version (though now only extant in its English and Latin derivatives) has the author submitting his book for approval to the Pope at Rome, but the papal court did not return to Rome from Avignon until 1377.[28]

None of these six references offers a convincing argument for believing that *Mandeville's Travels* was not, as the author states, written in 1357 or thereabouts. And acceptance of this date *c.* 1357 is now common ground among Mandeville scholars.

26 Thomas.
27 Warner ed., *op. cit.*, p. xxix.
28 Sisam pp. 239–40.

Provenance

The place of composition of *Mandeville's Travels* is unknown. In the prologue the author states:

> sachies qe ie eusse cest liuret mis en latin pour plus briefment deuiser. Mais pour ce qe pluseurs entendent mieulx rommant qe latin, ie lay mis en rommant par quoy qe chascun lentende. (p. 231)

It is possible that this claim could have been made in England *c.* 1357. French was then the language of the Court and the law, and the *Polychronicon*, chapter 59 of Ralph Higden (d. 1364) attested its widespread usage; though when Trevisa translated the chronicle in 1387 he reported that the teaching of French was being abandoned since the Black Death of 1349,[29] and this decline is emphasised by the eight translations (four into Latin, four into English) of *Mandeville's Travels* made in England before 1400. However, the dominance of French over Latin in France and its north-eastern borderlands was always unchallenged, and the author's desire to reach a wider public by writing *en rommant* makes better sense in such a geographical context. Le Long's translations of Latin itineraries into French in 1351 offer an exact parallel of time and place and matter. No certainty of provenance, then, can be pressed from this statement of preference for writing in French though, significantly perhaps, it is unaccompanied by a record of his place of writing and so may be deliberately ambiguous.

Equally ambiguous is a single reference to Liège which occurs in the Continental Version (but not in the Insular Version) in Chapter 11 where Aix-la-Chapelle is said to lie *a viii. lieues de Liege* (p. 273). None of the author's sources at this point refer to Liège. The reference may indicate some local connexion, though the dominance of the city of the Prince Bishops over the region was, of course, not merely local knowledge; or it may derive from a scribal interpolation made very early in the scribal tradition, possibly citing Liège as a depository of other relics. In either case the stated distance of Aix-la-Chapelle (now Aachen) is approximately accurate; the French league was roughly equivalent to three English miles, and the distance as the crow flies is about 25 miles (40 kilometres).

An examination of the sources which the author used in compiling his book is more rewarding. The precise number of these is an area of dispute where analogues, like William of Rubruck, *Historia Mongolorum*, 1255 and Marco Polo, *Le divisament dou Monde*, 1299, are sometimes cited as sources without irrefutable proof. The author's use of the following main sources, however, is uncontroversial:

29 Sisam p. 149.

Twelfth and thirteenth centuries

Albert of Aix, *Historia Hierosolimitana*, 1125
Brunetto Latini, *Le livre dou tresor*, c. 1264
Jacques de voragine, *Legenda aurea*, c. 1275
Jacques de Vitry, *Historia Hierosolimitana*, before 1240
Pseudo-Odoric, *De terra sancta*, c. 1250
Letter of Prester John, c. 1165
Peter Comestor, *Historia scholastica*, before 1179
Vincent of Beauvais *Speculum historiale*, c. 1250, which includes lengthy
    extracts from John of Plano Carpini, *Historia Mongolorum*
John Sacrobosco, *De sphera*, c. 1220
William of Tripoli, *De statu Saracenorum*, 1270

Fourteenth century

Directorium ad faciendum passagium transmarinum, c. 1330
Haiton, *La flor des estoires de la terre d'Orient*, before 1308
Odoric, *Itinerarius*, 1330
William of Boldensele, *Itinerarium*, 1337

Several of these works and others of comparable interest were translated into French in the second quarter of the fourteenth century. Thus, one volume written in Paris c. 1350 (now British Library MS. Royal 19 D. i) contains French versions of the *Historia de proelis* and the *Vengeance d'Alexandre*, Marco Polo, Odoric, the extracts from Carpini concerning the Mongols found in Vincent of Beauvais, *Speculum historiale*, and the *Directorium*; the last three of these translations being the work of Jean de Vignay (d. c. 1342), a Hospitaller of the Italian Order of St Jacques de Haut Pas, then living at the French house in Paris. And Jean le Long's translations, partly indebted to Jean de Vignay, of Haiton, Odoric, William of Boldensele, Ricold of Monte Croce, an account of the Great Khan by the archbishop of Sultanieh, and some letters from the Khan to Pope Benedict XII, were completed in 1351. 'Mandeville', who used le Long's work, may well have used other contemporary French translations of these sources, and it is worth remarking that when he compiled his own travel book in French c. 1357, he was writing in a well-established literary tradition.

Such a large and expensive collection of books, in Latin and in French translation, could only have been found c. 1357 in a major ecclesiastical or academic library. The admittedly incomplete but well-researched records of English libraries at this time provide several examples of the sources listed above which were written before 1300, with the exception of the Letter of Prester John in the recension used by 'Mandeville' which is not recorded in

England at all.[30] But there is no trace of any of the later sources listed, in Latin or in French translation, in England in the first half of the fourteenth century. Indeed, the only copy of le Long's translation known to have been in England before 1500 was written *c.* 1450,[31] at approximately the time of writing of the only known English copy of the *Directorium* (now Magdalen College, Oxford, MS. 43). Bibliographic argument in such a context is necessarily incomplete, but these tentative pointers towards a non-English origin are supported by the absence of any reference to Bartholomaeus Anglicus, *De proprietatibus rerum*, *c.* 1245 (which contained the most comprehensive descriptions of countries then available) and to Higden, *Polychronicon*, *c.* 1347, both widely available in English libraries at that time.[32] The failure to use these two recognised English authorities is inexplicable if *Mandeville's Travels* were compiled in England. Indeed, so widespread was the national reputation of the *Polychronicon* that in one Latin interpolation concerning the submission of the book to the Pope at Rome it is stated to be the authority by which 'Mandeville' is confirmed.[33]

The evidence offered by the sources, together with the author's stated preference for writing *en rommant*, suggests the likelihood that *Mandeville's Travels* was compiled in a Continental ecclesiastical library in a French-speaking area which had acquired a copy of le Long's translations within six years of its completion in 1351. The investigation of such libraries in France and adjacent regions in the north-west and their contents *c.* 1357 is far advanced but not yet brought to a systematic conclusion.[34] Consequently, any large ecclesiastical library within these regions offers the possibility of hypothesis, be it at Paris or Liège or elsewhere. The dissemination and language of the early manuscripts point to Paris and its regions as a probable centre of production, but whether this centre was also the point of origin is uncertain. At best, one can infer that *Mandeville's Travels* was written in an ecclesiastical library in northern or north-eastern France.

30 N.R. Ker, *Medieval libraries of Great Britain* (2nd ed., 1964) and its *Supplement*, ed. A.G. Watson (1987).

31 British Library MS. Cotton Otto D. i.

32 M.C. Seymour, 'Some medieval English owners of *De proprietatibus rerum*', *Bodleian Library Record* ix (1974), pp. 156–65 and J. Taylor, *The 'Universal Chronicle' of Ralph Higden* (1966). The *Polychronicon* was always rare on the Continent; see *Speculum* 42 (1963), p. 193.

33 Seymour ed., *Bodley Version* (1963), p. 175.

34 See A Vernet, *Histoire des bibliothèques français*, Vol. 1 *Les bibliothèques médiévales* (1989); and A. Genevois *et al.*, *Bibliographie des manuscrits médiévaux en France relevé des inventaires du VIIIe au XVIIIe siècle* (1987).

The nationality of the author

At the beginning of the work the author claims to be an Englishman:

> ie Iehan de Mandeuille, cheualier, ia soit ce chose que ie ne seie mie dignes,
> nez et nourris dengleterre de la ville de Saint Aubin, qui passay le mer lan
> m. ccc. xxii. le iour de Saint Michiel. (p. 231)

This claim is supported by a number of overtly English references in the text. The first of these occurs in Chapter 15 where, having transcribed a form of the 'Arabic' alphabet in his account of the Saracens, the author writes:

> nous auons en nostre langaige en Engleterre deux lettres plus quil ny a en
> abc, cest assauoir 3 et þ. (p. 309)

These Middle English letters *yogh* and *thorn* were widely known throughout the Continent through the common exchange of persons on embassies, trade, and other public and private expeditions, including the return of French prisoners held captive in England for ransom. An awareness of them cannot be construed as a confirmation of nationality. It may be. On the other hand, it may be simply a device to encourage credibility, like the author's demonstrably false claims to have travelled through the Valley Perilous in the company of two friars (Friar Odoric being his source at that point) and to have calculated the circumference of the globe (properly the work of Eratosthenes, quoted by Vincent of Beauvais) *selon la petitece de mon sens*.

Another English reference is merely a gloss on *eder que nous appellons yvy* which occurs in the account of the castle of the sparrowhawk in Chapter 16 (p. 311) and also in the account of the pepper forest in Chapter 18 (p. 325); neither gloss is found in the Insular Version. Whether it is a genuine gloss by the author or a scribal interpolation is unclear, for such glosses added by scribes at random in the later Middle Ages are not by any means unknown. Whatever its origins, the glosses do add some English colouring to the book, but since an acquaintance with the English word *ivy*, like the letters 3 and þ, was not confined to Englishmen, they too cannot be construed as proof of nationality.

A more explicit claim to Englishness is made in Chapter 18:

> nous sommes en i. climat qui est de la lune, et la lune est de legier
> mouuement et si est planete de voie. Et pour ce elle nous donne matere et
> uolente de mouuoir legierement et de cheminer par diuerses voies et de
> cerchier choses estranges et le diuerses choses du mond. (p. 321)

This national reputation for restlessness dates from the appearance of English mercenaries in the Varangian Guard after the disaster at Hastings in 1066, and is so supported by a constant stream of English pilgrims, crusaders, and scholars to Europe and the Holy Land that it is reported by Gower among others.[35] Clearly, it is something of a *topos* and as such admirably apposite in a travel book allegedly written by an Englishman, but it cannot be considered as proof of the author's nationality.

There are several other, apparently casual references to an English heritage (to Richard I, Edward I, the shrine of St James of Compostela, pp. 247, 328), but all were within common knowledge and none of contemporary notice. The one investigator who accepts their credibility without qualification writes of them:

> These are artful notes on Englishry, if they were put in to sustain the pretense that the author was an Englishman, but they would be natural enough if he really was an Englishman.[36]

Just so. But there are also two other statements in the book which, in conjunction with the many demonstrably false claims that the author makes on his own behalf in other contexts, cast doubt on his veracity in this regard.

The first is the claim that he is an English knight *nez et nourris dengleterre de la ville de Saint Aubin.* English gentry were occasionally born in towns but they were never bred there. The whole structure of feudalism was based on their living on their estates, and the custom of sending sons at an early age into the households of others superior in the social hierarchy was so well established that the concept of such a son's being raised in the town of his birth is without historical parallel. Even if the phrase *nez et nourris* is regarded as an alliterative legal or literary collocation, the author's use of it is clearly intended to mislead.

The second reason to doubt the author's claim to be English is more precise. When he refers to the stone bearing the imprint of the left foot of Jesus when he ascended to heaven which was revered as a relic in the chapel of Mount Olivet (p. 281), he fails to mention, in contrast to his general practice of referring to rival and often duplicate claims of various churches and shrines to possess identical relics, another stone bearing the imprint of the right foot which was given to Henry III (d 1272) and displayed at Westminster abbey from 1249, rivalling in sanctity the phial of holy blood at Hailes abbey as the most venerated relic in the kingdom. So remarkable is this omission that it is rectified by the maker of the Metrical Version, himself indisputably an Englishman of the north:

> That oþer stone is in Engelond here

35 Gower, *Confessio Amantis* VII. 749–54.
36 Bennett, *Rediscovery*, p. 177.

In the abbeie of Westmynstere.[37]

It is not credible that any man, born and bred in St Albans, a town domi-
nated by its Benedictine abbey, should not have known of so celebrated a
relic displayed within a twenty mile distance, and that, knowing of it, should
fail to mention it in defiance of his normal practice.

The fiction of nationality is made the more obvious by the author's as-
sumption of the name 'Sir John Mandeville'. The descendants of Geoffrey
de Mandeville flourished throughout the kingdom after the Conquest, and
there are historical records of several John Mandevilles in the thirteenth and
fourteenth centuries. But detailed searching and argument intent on locating
a Sir John Mandeville born at St Albans c. 1300 (the latest approximate date
of birth of one who must have attained his majority before leaving the
kingdom in 1322) has failed to discover any trace of him. And all posthumous references in England to 'Sir John Mandeville' the author of his book,
which begin with the chronicles of Thomas de Burton and Thomas
Walsingham, both writing before 1396, reflect the claims of the book without offering any additional information, which is a cogent argument that such
information was never available in England, especially as Walsingham was
writing at St Albans itself.[38] Even the most ardent advocate of a genuine Sir
John Mandeville as author of the work was forced to conclude her investigations and speculations:

In the end we know no more about him than he tells us in his book.[39]

Just so, but in the end he tells us that he was not an Englishman and that
his name was not 'Sir John Mandeville'.

Why the author adopted such a pseudonym remains a matter of speculation. It was a name of some dignity, with an authentic aristocratic association but not remarkable enough to require a detailed lineage, and it denoted
a member of the nation which, after the victories at Crécy in 1346 and
Poitiers in 1356, seemed to dominate France. There was even a genuine John
Mandeville in Edward III's army at Crécy in 1346 who returned with the
king to Calais in October 1355 and may have unconsciously lent his name.[40]
More likely, it was the imaginative choice of a well-known name from a

37 Seymour ed., *Metrical Version* (1973), p. 32, lines 1166–7.

38 Thomas de Burton, *Chronica*, ed. E.A. Bond (Rolls Ser. 1886–8) III. 158; and Thomas
Walsingham, *Annales*, ed. H.T. Riley (Rolls Ser. 1871) II. 306.

39 Bennett, *Rediscovery*, p. 216.

40 G. Wrotlesley, 'Crécy and Calais. From the Public Records', *Collections... William Salt
Arch. Soc.* xviii (1897), p. 238. On this John Mandeville of Beelsby, Lincs. see Bennett,
Rediscovery, pp. 188–9. Boston Public Library, Boston, Mass. MS. 1519 lists the retinue of
Edward III at the siege of Calais, 3 Sept. 1346 to 3 Aug. 1347.

restless race; and if so, it was an inspired one, for it passed the muster of credibility for hundreds of years. Yet, as always with *Mandeville's Travels*, there is an intriguing possibility that it may have had a literary origin. There appeared in France *c.* 1340 a satiric romance, *Le roman de Mandevie*, in which a *noble chevalier nomme Mandevie* leads the reader through an imaginary moral world, echoing the footsteps of Virgil, Dante and the future Chaucer, in much the same way that 'Mandeville' guides the reader through the terrestrial world.[41] The home of this noble knight is on a *blanche montaigne*, in Latin *mons albus*. Both names, *Mandevie* and *mons albus*, are teasingly close to *Mandeville* and *St Albans*, and the temptation to link them becomes the greater when it is discovered that the date 'Mandeville' gives for his departure may also have a literary origin.

'Mandeville' claims to have left England on Michaelmas 1322, a surprisingly precise date for which there are no parallels in the book. The port of departure during the reign of Edward II (1284–1327) was Dover, and in the aftermath of the defeat of Thomas of Lancaster at Boroughbridge 16 March 1322 it was strictly guarded. The feast of Michaelmas, 29 September, fell on a Wednesday that year. Later September is a time of equinoctial gales in the English channel, but there are no records of shipping movements or weather for that day to confirm whether or not a passage to France was possible.

One of the major sources for the account of the Holy Land in *Mandeville's Travels* is the *Itinerarium* written after his return in 1336 by the German knight Wilhelm von Boldensele at the instance of Cardinal Talleyrand-Périgord, then at the papal court at Avignon and the patron of Petrarch. Boldensele dated his dedicatory preface to Peter abbot of Aula Regiae

Auinione anno domini millesimo trecentesimo tricesimo septimo in die sancti Michaelis.[42]

This *Itinerarium* was translated by Jean le Long in 1351, and that translation was used by 'Mandeville', possibly alongside the original. All extant manuscripts of le Long's translation read *m. iii. xxxvii.* here, but 'Mandeville' may have used a copy which had *m. iii. xxii.*; cf. the variation of dates of departure, expressed in roman numerals, in the English versions of *Mandeville's Travels*, 1300, 1302, 1312, 1322, 1332, 1333. What appears beyond reasonable coincidence is the occurrence in both source and book

41 *Roman de Mandevie et les Melancholies de Jean du Pin*, ed. L. Karl (1913) and Karl's articles in *Revue des langues romans* 63 (1926), pp. 297–302 and 71 (1951), p. 69–70; Warner ed., *op. cit.*, pp. xxxix–xl.

42 Boldensele, *Itinerarium*, ed. C.L. Grotefend (1887), p. 237. Jean le Long's translation of Boldensele is edited by C. Deluz (Sorbonne thesis, privately printed 1972).

of the reference to *die sancti Michaelis*. In the context of similarly contrived disguises of his sources it seems certain that 'Mandeville' began his imaginary travels on the day that Boldensele completed his record of his own genuine travels.

The account of Egypt and the Holy Land

In his descriptions of Egypt and the Holy Land 'Mandeville' follows mainly the accounts of Boldensele 1337 and the Pseudo-Odoric *c.* 1250, which are supplemented by many other pilgrim records, like those of Haiton, Jacques de Vitry, Thietmar, William of Tripoli. In accordance with his usual method he conflates and inflates these accounts into his own allegedly first-hand report. The bulk of his information can be traced, readily enough, to the writers mentioned above, but some few details cannot. For example, at the end of a list of the Ayyubid and Mamluk sultans of Egypt (which is otherwise wholly derived from Haiton's account which ended at 1307 when Malik al-Nasir, d. 1341, was sultan) he adds the names of two successors, *Melechmader* and *Melechinam Damron* (p. 248), saying that the latter murdered the former and was the sultan when he left Egypt. If these names, despite the wide variation of different spellings in the manuscripts, can be identified with the immediate historical heirs of al-Nasir, i.e. al-Mansur murdered by his brother al-Ashraf who was himself murdered in 1342, it can be argued that 'Mandeville' left Egypt in 1341/2.[43] Alternatively, he could have heard these names from the lips of a traveller. In similar fashion, 'Mandeville' records some minor details, like the number of columns and

---

43 Warner ed., *op. cit.*, p. xviii suggests 'Melik-'Imád-ed-deen and Melik-el-Mudhaffar', the fourth and sixth sons. In his list of the caliphs for the Mamluk sultanate Atiya, *op. cit.*, p. 534 transliterates the names of the sons of al-Mustakfi Nasir thus:

1340　al-Mansur Sayf-al-Dīn Abu-Bakr
1341　al-Ashraf 'Alā'-al-Dīn Qujuq
1342　al-Nāsir Shibāb-al-Dīn Ahmad
1342　al-Sālih 'Imād-al-Dīn Ismā'īl
1345　al-Kāmil Sayf-al-Dīn Sha'ban
1346　al-Muẓaffar Sayf-al-Dīn Hajjī
1347　al-Nāsir-al-Dīn Hassan
1351　al-Sālih Salah-al-Dīn Sālih.

M. Ross, *Rulers and Governments of the World*, vol. 1 (1978), p. 55 lists only three: 4 May 1340 al Wathiq, 18 June 1340 al-Hakim II, July–August 1352 al-Mu'tadid. Difficulties of transliteration and dating within the Christian system, as well as scribal corruption within the textual traditon of *Mandeville's Travels*, make identification hazardous. Haiton's list of the Ayyubid sultans and the Mamluk caliphs (in Jean le Long's version) is given by L. de Baecker, *L'extrême Orient au Moyen Age* (1877), pp. 226–31.

steps in the Church of the Nativity at Bethlehem,[44] which are not found in his known sources but are confirmed by later travellers, the Seigneur d'Anglure in 1395, Poloner in 1422, Felix Fabri in 1481; though these may, of course, have been influenced by 'Mandeville' or successively by each other.

The first in modern times to accept, on such evidence and the general ground of its credibility, that 'Mandeville' did indeed visit these lands was one of the two scholars who discovered the sources of the book,[45] and his authority has lent credence and encouragement to those who believe in a historical knight-pilgrim. Others who deny this possibility have argued that such details reported by 'Mandeville' but not found in his known sources may derive from accounts as yet undiscovered or no longer extant and from verbal reports of genuine travellers.

There are, however, a number of errors and anachronisms in these chapters that cast doubt on the possibility that 'Mandeville' was reporting anything from his own observation. Thus, he claims falsely that a spear set in the ground in Jerusalem at the spring and autumn equinox casts no shadow (p. 333). When following the Pseudo-Odoric c. 1250 he visits Calvary, he fails to report the notable relic of Adam's skull on display there since at least 1330.[46] He describes the church of Mount Sion (p. 277) which Symeon Simeonis reported in ruins in 1323, and likewise the church of St Chariton (p. 268) which Ludolph von Sudheim reported completely in ruins in 1336; neither church was rebuilt in the fourteenth century.[47] When following Boldensele, who travelled northwards on this sector of his journey, he lists the towns en route from Gaza to Athlit, he preserves Boldensele's order while himself claiming to be travelling southwards. He claims that he fought against the Bedouin, a pastoral people who, he says, live wholly by hunting and cook their fish by the sun, a detail which Vincent of Beauvais reports of the Ichthyophagi on the Red Sea (p. 263).

Moreover, *Mandeville's Travels* was demonstrably compiled in a library and it is hard to imagine that as the author combined the many details of this source and that into his own compilation, he occasionally added a few, very precise remembrances from his own very clear memory. Such clarity of recall becomes even more unlikely when it appears that overall his account of these lands adds nothing to our knowledge of them in the fourteenth century:

44 Warner ed., *op. cit.*, p. 177, n. to 35/17; Bennett, *Rediscovery*, p. 59.

45 Bovenschen pp. 305–6.

46 Warner ed., *op. cit.*, p. 178.

47 Symeon Symeonis, *Itinerarium*, ed. M. Esposito (1960), p. 111. Ludolph von Sudheim, *De itinere terre sancte*, ed. F. Deycks (1851), p. 93.

The marvel is that if, as he states, he visited Jerusalem many times, he has contributed so little to our knowledge of it.[48]

There seems no valid reason for believing that the description of these lands is based on anything more than the books and possibly the oral reports of other men and the creative art of the compiler.

This lack of first-hand information is also evident in the lack of knowledge of Arabic displayed in *Mandeville's Travels*. The Saracen alphabet given at the end of Chapter 15 (pp. 308–9) owes the names of its letters to Aethicus, *Cosmographia*, quoted (with Hebrew, Greek, and Runic) by Hrabanus Maurus, *De inventione linguarum*, before 856, and its forms to Runic which have been re-arranged from the *futhorc* to follow the order of the Roman alphabet.[49] The Arabic words which appear in the text, in variously corrupt forms (here recorded according to the transliteration system of *New Arabian Studies*), are all derived from known written sources: *almās* 'diamond', *balsam* 'balsam', *filfil* 'pepper', *fusṭāṭ* 'tent', *ḥurmah* 'holiness', *karrah* 'attack', *malik* 'sultan', *maṣḥaf* 'book', *maydān* 'square, market-place', *masjid* 'mosque', *zarāfah* 'giraffe'. The quotation of the *shahāda* (*La ilāha illa 'illāhu wa-Muḥammadun rasūlu 'illāhi* 'there is but one God and Muhammad is his prophet'), and the relics of Arabic words found in names and titles (e.g. *Calahelit* p. 246 denoting the citadel of Cairo and *Galcat* p. 388, variant *Galchalonabes* in the Insular Version, denoting the leader of the Assassins *Shaykhu 'l-jibal* 'sheikh of the mountains'; both have as their first element *qal'ah*, colloquial *gal'ah* 'fortress') have a similarly bookish origin.[50]

Despite his claim to have travelled widely in Arab lands and to have served the Sultan in Egypt for many years (p. 246), 'Mandeville' clearly has no personal knowledge of Arabic. This ignorance is a further argument against his claims to report at first hand. There can be no doubt that he did not visit Egypt and the Holy Land.[51]

It may be worth remarking here that the author's knowledge of other exotic languages is equally dependent on written sources. The Greek alphabet, like the Saracen, is taken from Hrabanus Maurus, and the two Greek quotations are from Peter Comestor and a derivative (pp. 412, 269). Hebrew occurs only in corrupt forms of place-names: *Beṣalél* 'in the shadow of God', *Me'arat* 'the cave', *Me'arat ha-Machpela* 'the cave of Machpela'. The few Mongol words derive from Carpini: *tuman* 'ten thousand', *Serai* 'palace', *Orda* 'camp', *ki-di-fou* 'inn-keeper'.

---

48 Warner ed., *op. cit.*, p. xx.
49 G.D. Painter in Letts 1949, pp. 154, 156–7.
50 Warner ed., *op. cit.*, pp. 193, 168, 216.
51 Fazy gives a contrary view.

The geography

In Chapter 20 'Mandeville' sets out his ideas of the world as a physical entity, having previously made passing and not always consistent references to its features. There are two traditions in his geography. First is the common medieval idea of the world depicted in the *Mappa mundi* and elsewhere which has its geographical centre at Jerusalem, to which and from which one travelled 'up' and 'down' over the bulge of the earth. Surrounding this centre were the three continents of Europe, Asia, and Africa, each with a Mediterranean littoral; and surrounding these landmasses was the Great Ocean Sea in which were many islands.

The second tradition adopted by 'Mandeville' is the Ptolemaic concept of the world as symmetrical globe with a circumference of approximately 20425 miles, around which it was possible, in theory at least, to sail from one landmass to another. According to this system, the world had seven 'climates', i.e. zones distinguished by the varying lengths of their longest day. Lands like England and Ceylon, not included in these zones (roughly between 16° 30' S and 50° 30' N) by the early geographers, were added in the Middle Ages to the most northerly and southerly zones without further distinction. Each of the seven climates was governed by one of the seven planets (e.g. England by the restless Moon and Ceylon by sluggish Saturn) and from such influences came the dispositions of the inhabitants. No uninhabitable 'torrid' zone separated north and south, and in the Antipodes men lived and walked on the surface of the earth exactly as those in northern climates. Medieval commentators located Earthly Paradise within the equator.

The major source of these ideas is Sacrobosco, *De sphera mundi*, c. 1220, a comprehensive explanation of the Ptolemaic system, with additions from Macrobius and Alfraganus, within a traditional Christian framework, which was prescribed as a university text-book at Paris and decisively shaped late medieval cosmography.[52] In this regard, one investigator claims that 'Mandeville'

> writes as a man of university education, one indeed who must have studied at one time or another at the University of Paris.[53]

Such plausible speculation may not be necessary. Though he clearly had an informed interest in geography and had studied Sacrobosco, the *De sphera* and commentaries on it, like that of Cecco d'Ascoli (burned at Florence in 1317 for such presumption), and others (though not the *Directorium ad*

---

52 L. Thorndike, *The Sphere of Sacrobosco and its Commentators* (1949), pp. 81–5.
53 E.G.R. Taylor in Letts' edition of 1953, I. li.

faciendum passagium transmarinum, perhaps written by the Dominican John de Cora, later archbishop of 'Persia' in 1330 and certainly used by 'Mandeville') were known throughout Europe and a man could come by them outside Paris.[54] On the other hand, Paris was the major European university and its students included laymen and ecclesiastics of all types.

At all events the information in *Mandeville's Travels* is bookish, for it includes the impossible claims that Jerusalem is the centre of the world and, from an unresolved confusion of Christian and Ptolemaic theories, that the land of Prester John which 'Mandeville' claims to have visited is the Antipodes. Nevertheless, all of this geography is simply, plausibly, and (in its bookish context) intelligently set down and supported by some reports of star-shots, precisely calculated to degrees and minutes, which he claims to have taken himself by astrolabe, the ancient and medieval circular instrument with graduated rim and sights which projects a sphere onto a plane and so determines the altitude of a heavenly body. These star-shots are given in the context of some demonstrably false claims (e.g. the existence of a Pole Antarctic, the adoption of Eratosthenes' calculation of the circumference of the globe as a personal observation) and at their most southerly take 'Mandeville' to a latitude of 33° 16' S, roughly that of Cape Town and Sydney. The first three of these star-shots are of the northern hemisphere (sightings of the Polar Star in Brabant, Alemania, and Bohemia) and are likely to be genuine records which 'Mandeville' borrowed from a yet unidentified treatise on the astrolabe; the remainder concern observations of the non-existent Pole Antarctic and so are false: they are probably based on the *Directorium* where the Dominican author reports:

> Sicut multa loca et prouincias inueniens mensus polum arcticum habitata, quae extra maiorem latitudinem ultimi climatis esse constat, cum in illis locis polus arcticus plus quam quinquaginta duobus gradibus eleuetur quae est, ut praemittitur, maior climatum latitudo... Processi ultra meridiem ad locum ubi polum nostrum arcticum non videbam et videbam polum antarcticum circa viginti quatuor gradus eleuatum. Ab isto loco ulterius non processi. Mercatores vero et homines fide digni passim ultra versus meridiem procedebant usque ad loca ubi asserebant polum antarcticum quinquaginta quatuor gradus eleuari.[55]

54 Manuscripts of *De sphera* and commentaries on it, like that of Michael Scot, are common. But the *Directorium* was not, it would appear, widely known; only three 15c. Latin copies are extant. 'Mandeville' may have used de Vignay's translation; see p. 9 above.

55 *Directorium, American Historical Review* 12 (1907) p. 821. Odoric visited Sumatra, which lies across the Equator. C.R. Beazley, *The Dawn of Modern Geography* (1906) III. 28. 133, 145, 264 etc. reports medieval knowledge of lands further south. The *polum antarcticum* reported here was probably Canopus, after Sirius the brightest star in the sky and visible only below latitude 37° N.

Neither genuine nor false calculations show any personal knowledge of the astrolabe;[56] rather, they are figures pressed into the service of the theory of a symmetrical globe, derived from Sacrobosco, and into substantiating the claim that 'Mandeville' has observed all but a small sector of the heavens:

> ainsi ne faut il que ie nay veu tout le firmament que iii. vins et iiii. degres et bien la moitie dun degre. Et ce nest mie la quatre partie de firmament. (p. 333)

Significantly, this alleged use of the astrolabe is confined to the one chapter of *Mandeville's Travels* which is concerned with the theory of the globe, and the latitudes of all the other exotic places which the author claims to have visited or passed by, not least the Earthly Paradise (p. 404), are unrecorded. Such omissions are not credible if the author were a genuine traveller interested in the stars and having an instrument with him, and his claim to have used an astrolabe on his journeys is worthless.

The orthodoxy of the book

The cosmography of the book is presented within a standard, almost unremarkable Christian orthodoxy of the fourteenth century. 'Mandeville' quotes the Bible forty-eight times (including eleven citations of the Psalms, ten of Matthew, eight of Luke, five of John, three of Job) and everywhere shows a detailed knowledge of its contents. He quotes Augustine twice and cites the *Vitas Patrum* once. The prologue shows that the author's foremost concern was the maintenance of the Christian faith, and there he reports the evils of simony and the avarice of Pope John XII (d. 1334); neither would have been a credible concern of a man who had just returned from a voyage of thirty-five years *in partibus infidelium*. Later, he reports contemporary criticism of Christian living through the device of the Sultan's colloquy (pp. 305–6), and puts forward the idea, supported by quotations from the Psalms, that all men of all persuasions have by the grace of God some inkling of the True Faith and need only missionaries to bring them to a full understanding (p. 410). This charity contrasts sharply with the informed prejudices of genuine travellers, like Carpini and William of Rubruck who were articulately unamused by the Tartars, appalled as much by their filthy habits as their pagan rites. 'Mandeville', of course, writing in the serenity of his library, had the inestimable advantage of never having lived among the heathens he describes.[57]

---

56 Gerritsen.

57 One exception to this general intolerance is Burchard of Mount Sion, *Descriptio terre sancte*, ed. J.C.M. Laurent, *Peregrinatores medii aevii quatuor* (1864).

This tolerance is extended to those of his faith. With the exceptions of simonists, popes, and the generally immoral noted above, about which there was universal agreement, he says not one partisan word in a century wracked by heresy and schism. Even the troubles of St Athanasius (d. 373) are recounted without one word about the Arian heresy which prompted them, and the rival claims of Amiens and Genoa to possess the severed head of the Baptist are gently reconciled in perfect simplicity:

> et en font les Geneuois grant fest. Et mesmes les Sarrazins en font fest de li. Aucuns dient que le chief Saint Iehan est a Amiens en Picardie; et les autres dient que cest chief Saint Iehan leuesque. Ie ne scay; Dieu le scet. Mais quelle part que on face a li honneur, le bon Saint Iehan le prent bien en gre. (p. 287)

Faith and charity can go no farther.

This knowledge of the Bible, concern for the faith, and serenity of outlook, strongly suggest a member of a religious order, untouched by the irksome problems of a factious humanity. This suggestion is reinforced by the *ordinatio* of the book, which is everywhere easily controlled and coherent and reflects an ordered, intellectual training, learned but not scholastic. The author's piety is not in doubt. As he says of his passage through the Valley Perilous,

> toutefuoies les bons Crestiens qui sont en estat estable et en vraye foy et creance y entrent bien senz peril. (p. 390)

And there is no reason to doubt the sincerity of his final prayer, conventional though it is, that his readers and auditors shall pray for him that God may forgive his sins. To combine diverse accounts of the Holy Land and *partes infidelium* into one easily comprehended book, and to release those accounts from their learned Latin into the more widely intelligible *doulx franceys*, so that all men might understand the diversity of humanity and the handiwork of God, was a charitable office and deserved the prayers of the faithful.

This essential piety is not disturbed by the shell of fantasy that surrounds the book. No doubt, 'Mandeville' took much quiet pleasure in constructing the *persona* of 'Sir John Mandeville', and equally, no doubt, in the common experience of the writer this *persona* exercised its influence on the book, leading him to confess his unworthiness to visit the Earthly Paradise (p. 405) and his unwillingness to visit the cannibal giants (p. 393), to add those artfully contrived touches of Englishness, and to expand imaginatively on his sources. Yet he also takes pains to alter and explain those sources where they seemed to him wrong-headed or lacking in detail. Thus, in spite of

Boldensele, he denies that the Pyramids are tombs and that horses can cross
the desert; to Odoric's account of the intense heat and the stitched ships in
the Gulf of Hormuz[58] in Chapter 18 he adds the explanations that the people survive by standing in the rivers and that magnetic rocks prevent the
use of iron; to Odoric's account of the Assassin paradise he adds the fairest
youths alongside the fairest damsels and puts underground the conduits
feeding the three fountains of milk, wine, and honey (p. 388) to enhance
the magic of the gardens; to Carpini's report, incorporated in Vincent of
Beauvais, of the Tartar habit of pickling the ears of the enemies (for the
sake of preserving them) he adds the explanation that they then served them
to their lords as a delicacy. A similar desire to explain on 'rational' grounds
is found in the thirteenth-century encyclopedists, all in regular orders, and
points to a basically serious approach to the matter of *Mandeville's Travels*.

Those who think otherwise have variously described the work as a hoax,
a forgery, a plagiarism, a romance, and so forth, but all such views are
anachronisms imposed on the book without regard to the author's intentions
and his context. The first half of the book (Chapters 1–15) is a factual account of the Holy Land and the ways thither, livelier than most because of
the framework provided by its fictional narrator but nonetheless as piously
informative as the rest of such itineraries and responding like them to the
attractions of the novel and the marvellous, as 'Mandeville' himself recog-
nizes:

> on dit tousiours et voir est que choses nouvelles plais et si les ot on volentiers.
> (p. 411)

The second half (Chapters 16–34) is a more imaginative account of the exotic
East of the Great Khan, Prester John, and their empires. The freshness and
vitality of their descriptions balance the greater and more familiar details of
the account of the Holy Land, but are still firmly based on the careful reports of genuine travellers and 'authorities' like Vincent of Beauvais and the
Letter of Prester John. The device of the fictional narrator binds the whole
together but is never obtrusive. From beginning to end *Mandeville's Travels*
is a popularly presented and seriously intended description of the wonders
of the world.

---

58 Marco Polo reported that the planks of Arab ships were fastened with cord made from
coir. A modern reconstruction of such a ship is described by T. Severin, *The Sindbad Voyage*
(1982), p. 20.

Conclusions

If this inquiry into the authorship of *Mandeville's Travels* is valid, a profile of its anonymous author can be assembled from its various parts. He was, then:

a) a native French-speaker, compiling his work *c*. 1357 in a large Continental library rich and active enough to acquire contemporary works within a few years of their composition. This library was, almost certainly, ecclesiastical and in northern France or Flanders;

b) an ecclesiastic, with a cleric's knowledge of the Bible, and most likely a member of a regular order;

c) a fluent reader of Latin, but without knowledge of Arabic or Greek;

d) an informed and intelligent reader of books describing the Holy Land and other exotic parts, capable of mastering the theories of Sacrobosco and his commentators, and alive to the possibilities of circumnavigating the world;

e) a man who had never travelled to the lands he describes.

He was also in touch with the Parisian book-trade and able to launch his own work into the mainstream of book-production.

There is one man who has such a profile, Brother Jean le Long (d. 1388) of the abbey church of St Bertin. Denied by the great Benedictine concept of *stabilitas* from travelling unless under dispensation for study or other good cause; widely read in accounts of foreign parts and experienced in making such Latin books available to those who knew only French; used to working in a large Benedictine library which, at the close of the Middle Ages, contained almost 800 manuscripts;[59] an inmate of a large Benedictine house at that time within the English administration and on the major route between Calais and Paris, where the abbot's hospitality, in accord with the Rule of St Benedict, was available to all who travelled the road, among them certainly English pilgrims from the Holy Land willing to recount their adventures to appreciative ears; and in a splendid geographical and professional position to introduce a new book to the major European centre of book-production at Paris; Jean le Long would be an ideal candidate for the authorship of *Mandeville's Travels*. There is, however, as yet nothing beyond conjecture to connect him directly with the work.

---

59 St Omer, Bibl. municipale MS. 813, an 18*c*. catalogue.

This lack of evidence may not always prevail. The library of St Bertin appears to have contained all the books which 'Mandeville' used in his compilation,[60] and a comparison of the style of le Long's known translations with that of *Mandeville's Travels* appears to offer some evidence of identity, though the absence of critical editions of both works prevents a definite conclusion.[61] Both lines of inquiry will repay the effort of study that is being devoted to them.

Meantime, one must keep an open mind. 'Mandeville' has been much exposed to identity-searchers, from Jean d'Outremeuse in his own day to the more ebullient writers of our own, and nothing except a possibility is put forward here. Yet whoever he was – and if he was not Jean le Long, he was clearly someone like him – an awareness of his shape or even perhaps his shadow is crucial to an understanding of his book. In the end 'Mandeville' matters.

---

60 *Ibid.* and H. Michelant and C. Duchet, *Catalogue sommaire des manuscrits de la ville de Saint-Omer* (1845), repeated in *Catalogue Générale des Manuscrits... des Départements* III (1861). *Histoire des bibliothèques françaises* I (1989), pp. 41, 47, 53 reports that about one hundred manuscripts survive with the ex libris *de librairie de Sancti Bertini.* Cf. A. Genevois *et al., Bibliothèques des manuscrits médiévaux en France* (1987), p. 213.

61 Such linguistic and rhetorical comparisons cannot be wholly straight-forward since le Long was a translator simply and 'Mandeville' much more of a composer, e.g. of his own syntax.

PART II. THE FICTIONS

The nature of the interpolations

The search for the author of *Mandeville's Travels* has been properly confined to the French book and so has screened from the quest the several false trails introduced by interpolators in dependent versions. The book was much given to interpolation. For example, the manuscripts of the Insular tradition in French, Latin, English, and Irish contain well over a hundred such additions. They are generally of two types, passages which bolster the authenticity of the original and passages which add marvels to the substance. In size they range from an emphatic statement of honesty, like

> Trowith this wel, for this haue I bothe herd and sen with mynne eyne and mynne eryn and myne felawys that were with me that weryn of dyuers regionys, for wete ye wel that al be it wondyr to youre heryng, I am not set to lye yow lesyngis. Trowith yif ye welyn,

(which occurs only in an abridgement of a lost English translation of a Latin recension of the Insular Version, i.e. at five major removes from the original work)[62] and a short description of an otherwise unknown 'ile of Hogge' in one English manuscript written on the Welsh border,[63] to lengthy accounts of Ultima Thule in the Egerton Version[64] and of Rome in the Metrical Version.[65]

Such interpolations often contain interesting material, like the spurious dedication to Edward III in some manuscripts of the Insular Version[66] and the account of the anachronistic visit to the Pope in Rome in the English manuscripts,[67] and are always seriously intended, particularly when they are Latin insertions into vernacular texts, like the letters of Sultan Balthazardy to the Pope in two Insular manuscripts[68] and the translation of the letter to

---

62 Seymour ed., *Bodley Version* (1963), p. 76.
63 British Library MS. Royal 17 B. xliii f. 70^{r-v}.
64 Warner ed., *op. cit.*
65 Seymour ed., *Metrical Version* (1973), pp. 4–14, lines 67–462.
66 Hamelius ed., *op. cit.*, II. 14. The dedication occurs in the ten mss. of subgroup 1 of the Insular Version and probably originated between 1360 and 1375; see p. 7 above.
67 Sisam pp. 238–40.
68 Hamelius ed., *op. cit.*, II. 40–2.

Alexander in some late English manuscripts.[69] Collectively, like the passages omitted by scribes and redactors and the various extracts and epitomes made throughout the fifteenth century, they tell a great deal about the way medieval readers saw *Mandeville's Travels*. But since all are easily recognized for what they are, they can be discounted as statements of the author without difficulty. There is, however, one series of interpolations so direct in its claims of authorship that it requires comment in any modern statement about 'Mandeville'.

The Liège interpolations

The Liège Version, a recension of the Continental Version and extant in seven manuscripts, is distinguished by a number of interpolations concerning Ogier le Danois, one of Charlemagne's legendary *douzpers*. In the epilogue of this version, after having claimed to have written his book from memory in his old age (as in the Continental Version), 'Mandeville' is made to state that he wrote:

> dedens la noble cyte de Lyege en la basse sabloniere (*va.* saveniere) en lostel Hannekin dit le volt a la requeste et proyere de honnorable (*va.* homme venerable) et discreit maistre Jehan de Bourgoigne dis a la barbe phizitien qui en ma maladie moy vizitoit, et en vizitant moy recognut et raviza sy com chil qui mavoyt veu en la court le souldan de Egypte avoec le quel il demoroyt quant je fuy la.[70]

This precision of detail is foreign to *Mandeville's Travel* but even more remarkable is its historicity. Hennequin le Volt was the proprietor of an *hôtel du Heaume* in la rue Basse Sauveniere from 3 August 1349 to his death in 1369, and Jean de Bourgogne (d. 1372) was a celebrated Liège physician who in 1365, when he wrote a well-known tract on the plague, stated that he had practised medicine *per 40 annos et amplius*.[71] The trigger for this suggestion of an earlier association of patient and physician is undoubtedly the claim by 'Mandeville' (p. 363) that the Sultan employed *bien cc. phisiciens qui sont tous Crestiens*.

From its detailed local knowledge the interpolation appears to have originated in Liège; it is unclear whether it was added to the Liège Version or always an integral part of it. Its date, clearly within living memory of Hennequin le Volt and presumably shortly after the death of Jean de

---

69 Extant in the mss. of subgroup 5 of the Defective Version.

70 De Poerck 1961, p. 39.

71 Jean de Bourgogne, *De pestilencia*, prologue (Bodleian Library MS. Ashmole 1443 f. 353). The Latin phrase is a medieval collocation denoting a long period of time rather than a literal '40 years and more'.

Bourgogne (unless he was party to the tale, which seems unlikely) was *c.* 1373. Because of the presence of references to Ogier le Danois, who features prominently in the chronicles of Jean d'Outremeuse (d. 1400 and aged 19 in 1357), a Liège notary in the service of the Prince Bishop, and because of the certain association of him with the later stages of this Mandeville interpolation, it is generally assumed that d'Outremeuse was responsible for the Liège Version and for this passage in it.[72] Such fictions which bring historical persons to Liège are found elsewhere in his works.[73]

This story of 'Mandeville's' residence in Liège is developed in the Latin translation of the Liège Version, extant in 38 manuscripts. In the account of Egypt 'Mandeville' is made to record the meeting with Jean de Bourgogne at the Sultan's court which is a feature of the earlier story:

> Porro ego in curia manens vidi circa soldanum unum venerabilem et expertum medicum de nostris partibus oriendum. Solebat namque circa se retinere diversarum medicos nationum, quos renominande audierit esse fame. Nos autem raro invicem convenimus ad colloquium, eo quod meum servicium cum suo modicum congruebat. Longo autem postea tempore et ab illo loco remote, videlicet in Leodii civitate composui hortatu et adiutorio eiusdem venerabilis viri hunc tractatum, sicut in fine huius tocius operis plenius enarrabo.[74]

And in the epilogue, translating and slightly altering the interpolation found at the end of the Liège Version, the Latin translation concludes:

> Itaque anno a nativitate domini Iesu Christi m. ccc. lv. in repatriando cum ad nobilem Legie seu Leodii civitatem permansissem et pre gravitate ac arteticis guttis illuc decumberem in vico qui dicitur basse sauenyr, consului causa convalescendi aliquod medicos civitatis et accidit dei nutu unum intrare phisicum super alios estate simul et canicie venerandum ac in sua arte euidenter expertum qui ibi dicebatur Iohannes ad barbam.
>
> Is ergo cum pariter colloqueremur interseruit dictis aliqua per que tam nostra invicem renovabatur antiqua noticia quam quondam habueramus in Cayr Egipti apud Calahelich soldani prout supra tetigi vii. capitulo huius libri.
>
> Qui cum in me experientiam artis sue excellenter monstrasset, adhortabatur ac precabatur instanter ut de his que videram tempora peregrinationis mee per mundum aliqua digererem in scriptis ad legendum et audiendum pro utilitate posteris.
>
> Sic quoque tandem illius monitiis et adiutorio compositus est iste tractatus de quo certe nihil scribere prosposueram donec saltem ad partes proprias in Anglia pervenissem.

72 De Poerck 1961, p. 48 dissents. But cf. Goosse 1968, pp. 248–50.

73 G. Kurth, *Étude critique sur Jean d'Outremeuse*, Académie royal de Belgique. Classe des lettres (Brussels 1910).

74 Hamelius ed., *op. cit.*, II. 5.

Et credo premissa circa me per providentiam et gratiam dei contigisse. Quum a tempore quo recessi duo reges nostri Anglie et Francie non cessaverunt invicem exercere prelia, destructiones insidias et interfectiones inter quas nisi a domino custoditus non transissem sine morte vel mortis periculo et sine criminum grandi cumulo. Et nunc ecce anno egressionis mee xxxiii. constitutus in Leodiensi civitate que a mari Anglie distat solum per duas dietas audio dictas dominorum inimicitias per gratiam dei compositas. Quapropter et spero ac propono de reliquo secundum maturiorem etatem me posse in propriis intendere corporis quieti animeque saluti.[75]

The reference to the Anglo-French treaty dates the passage to 1375. Time needed for the dissemination of the original French book c. 1357, its recension into the Liège Version c. 1373, and subsequent translation into Latin makes certain that the interpolator refers to the Truce of Bruges agreed in 1375 and not the earlier Truce of Brétigny, near Chartres, which was ratified at Calais 24 October 1360 and kept the peace until 1369.[76] Two other arguments support this reference, the proximity of Bruges to Liège and the death of Jean de Bourgogne in 1372 who thus could not object to fantasies which involved him.

Extraordinarily, the legend develops a third growth. In *Ly tresorier de philosophie naturelle des pierres precieuses*, which he wrote between 1382 and 1390, d'Outremeuse cites as one of his authorities

Jehan de Mandeville chevalier, seigneur de Montfort et de Castel Perouse, et de l'isle de Campdi.[77]

The titles of lordship are new, but otherwise the reference comes wholly from the Liège Version or its Latin translation. But then in the fourth book of *Ly myreur des histors*, begun c. 1388 and covering the years 1341 to 1399, d'Outremeuse developed the story even further:

L'an m. ccc. lxxii. mourut à Liège le 12 novembre un homme fort distingué par sa naissance, content de s'y faire connoitre sous le nom de Jean de Bourgogne dit à la barbe. Il s'ouvrit néanmoins au lit de la mort à Jean d'Outremeuse, son compère, et institué son exécuteur testamentaire. De vrai, il se titra dans le précis de sa dernière volonté messire Jean de Mandeville, chevalier comte de Monfort en Angleterre et seigneur de l'isle de Canpdi et du chasteau Perouse. Ayant cependant eu le malheur de tuer en son pays un comte qu'il ne nomme pas, il s' engagea à parcourir les trois parties du monde.

75 *Ibid.* pp. 5–6.
76 M. McKisack, *The Fourteenth Century* (1959), pp. 140–1, 145.
77 Bennett, *Rediscovery*, p. 98, n. 25.

Vint à Liège en 1343. Tout sorti qu'il étoit d'une noblesse très distinguée,
il aima de s'y tenir caché. Il étoit au reste grand naturaliste, profond
philosophe et astrologue, y joint en particulier une connaissance très singulière
de la physique, se trompant rarement lorsqu'il disoit son sentiment à l'égard
d'un maladie, s'il en reviendroit ou pas. Mort enfin, on l'enterra aux freres
Guillelmins au faubourg d'Avroy.[78]

This patent elaboration of the earlier story of Jean de Bourgogne's involve-
ment with *Mandeville's Travels* is wholly in keeping with the fanciful nature
of d'Outremeuse's chronicle. No member of the great Anglo-French crusading
family of Montfort ever carried the surname 'Mandeville', but elsewhere in
Ly myreur des histors d'Outremeuse falsely styles Simon de Montfort (killed
at Evesham 1265) *li conte de Monfort* and in extravagant and romantically
inflated terms describes the fortunes of several members of the family, giving
eleven of Simon's 'thirty' sons stalls in cathedrals at Liège and Cologne
(when, in fact, Amaury was the only one of his five sons to be a canon,
briefly at York Cathedral).[79]

With knowledge of d'Outremeuse's fascination with the Montfort family,
something can be unravelled from this 'Mandeville' legend. The titles of
lordship ascribed by him to 'Mandeville' have the authentic ring of petty
lordships of northern France and Burgundy.[80] The style of *comte de Monfort
l'Amauri* is historic, though never held by the English branch, and at the
end of the fourteenth century it was held by the dukes of Brittany. Montfort
l'Amauri lies five miles west of Rennes, and Perouse (now Bazouges-la-
Perouse) five miles to the north. No other references to the *seigneurie de
l'isle de Campdi* are known, but in the context the name is unlikely to be
an invention.[81]

The story of the murder of an unnamed count is likewise, in its origins,
part of the Montfort history. On 13 March 1271 Henry of Cornwall, thought
to have caused the mutilation of the body of Simon de Montfort after the
battle of Evesham, was pulled from a church at Viterbo in Italy by two of
Simon's sons and spectacularly hacked to death. Another son, Amaury, was

78 S. Bormann, *Ly Myreur des Histors* VII (1887) cxxxiii–iv, followed by R. Lejeune p.
418. The quotation, based on the lost fourth book of *Li Myreur*, is a summary in modern
French made by a Liège herald, Louis Abry (d. 1720).

79 D'Outremeuse, *Ly Myreur des Histors* V. 316, 368 and IV. 300 and the review of Goosse
in *Speculum* 19 (1965).

80 Cf. R. Vaughan, *John the Fearless* (1966), p. 56, which includes a map of the prin-
cipality of Liège. Another map is given by F.-L. Ganshof, *Étude sur le développement des
villes... au Moyen Age* (1943), map 18.

81 Bennett, *Rediscovery* p. 99, cf. Hamelius ed., *op. cit.*, II. 8. The form *disle* 'of the isle'
may be a false expansion of an abbreviated *domini* or some such.

falsely suspected of complicity in this murder and imprisoned by Edward I at Corfe; freed in 1282, he left England and lived in Paris and Italy, having previously studied medicine at Padua and earned a reputation as *clericus eminentis litteraturae*; he died in exile in 1295, the last of the male line.[82]

It is clear that d'Outremeuse had got hold of this story, in garbled or ungarbled form, and untroubled by chronology, decided to reveal the identity of the unknown 'Mandeville' as the well-born and reputed Amaury de Montfort. The context of this revelation was probably imaginary, but it is possible that d'Outremeuse was the executor of Jean de Bourgogne and may have witnessed his death-bed. At all events, the revelation was melodramatic enough to inspire further embellishments of the legend. But before considering them, it may be worth restating the three stages of the legend so far recovered: *c.* 1373 the Liège Version claims that 'Mandeville' met Jean de Bourgogne at Liège, both having previously served the Sultan in Cairo; in 1375/6 the Latin translation develops the claim that de Bourgogne urged 'Mandeville' to write down his account of the world; sometime after 1388 d'Outremeuse (d. 1400) claims first that 'Mandeville' wrote a lapidary and then that de Bourgogne was 'Mandeville'.

The apocryphal works

The spurious identification of 'Mandeville' with Jean de Bourgogne necessarily implied a single authorship for the former's French *Voyages* and the latter's Latin medical tracts, *De pestilencia* and two unidentified works mentioned therein, *De causa et natura corrupti aeris* and *De distinctione moribus moribus pestilentialium*.[83] Curiously, these medical tracts do not appear among the apocrypha attributed to 'Mandeville' in the last quarter of the fourteenth century. Instead, in pride of place is the lapidary which d'Outremeuse in his *Tresorier de philosophie* ascribes to

> ung noble homme seigneur Jehan de Mandeville, chevalier, seigneur de Montfort, de Castel Perouse et de l'isle de Campdi, qui fut en orient et es parties par della par long temps, si en fist ung lapidaire selon l'oppinion des Indois.[84]

D'Outremeuse claims to quote from this lapidary twelve times, but it has not been identified. The compilers of such tracts quoted verbatim from each

---

82 C. Bémont, *Simon de Montfort, Earl of Leicester 1208–1265* (trans. E. Jacob, 1930), pp. 260–6. *Flores historiarum* (Rolls Ser.) III. 67.

83 Jean de Bourgogne, *loc. cit.* which gives the incipits as *Deus deorum* and *Cum inuenitur*. D.W. Singer and A. Anderson, *A Catalogue of Latin and Vernacular Plague Tracts* (1950), pp. 26–48 lists the manuscripts of *De pestilencia*.

84 De Poerck 1961, p. 35, n. 1.

other, and often revised and expanded, collated and re-ordered their material, so that it is extremely difficult to be certain about the origins and originality of any lapidary.[85] D'Outremeuse refers three times to *Mandeville's Travels* in the *Tresorier*, and the account of the diamond which 'Mandeville' gives in Chapter 17 is presumably the trigger for the idea of such a lapidary, which is then embellished by a fanciful report of precious stones given to 'Mandeville' during a seven-year stay at Alexandria and later in d'Outremeuse's possession.[86] The lapidary which the *Tresorier* cites as that written by 'Mandeville' is wholly different from a small tract describing nine stones which is appended to one manuscript of the Liège Version and credited to 'Johans de mande ville chevalier' in the colophon but to 'maistre Johans a la barbe' in the *incipit*.[87]

Another lapidary attributed to 'Mandeville' occurs, much more impressively, with other apocryphal works in a copy of the Liège Version, Musée Condé, Chantilly MS. 699, thought to date before 1400.[88] Here the Liège text of 'Mandeville' is followed by four short tracts, also in French, which are attributed to him: ff. 75–88 a cosmography, ff. 88–96ᵛ a cosmology, ff. 96ᵛ–102ᵛ a herbal, ff. 102ᵛ–8ᵛ a lapidary. The last item, the only one of the four tracts in print,[89] differs from both lapidaries previously linked to 'Mandeville' (in the *Tresorier* and in the manuscript of 1461, cited above).

These four tracts are all the work of one man, jumbled, superstitious, uncritical, and making no contribution to the sciences which they claim to illuminate. Since they treat of 'Mandeville' in ways very similar to those of the *Tresorier* and are written in the same grandiose style, the presumption is that they are the work of d'Outremeuse,[90] and this is partly supported by a linguistic analysis of the manuscript which places the scribe within the area of Liège.[91] These apocrypha, though now uniquely extant, are copies of an earlier spurious 'collected works'; one other manuscript of the Liège Version, written in Liège in 1396, has the *explicit: le premier liure des cinq liures messier Jehan de mandeville*.[92] Since this manuscript is the oldest dated copy of the Liège Version, it is possible that the archetype of the 'collected works' pre-dated the *Tresorier* (*c.* 1382–90); but in that case it is difficult

85 Cf. M.C. Seymour, *Bartholomaeus Anglicus and his Encyclopedia* (1992), pp. 172–82.

86 D'Outremeuse, *Le tresorier de philosophie naturelle* (BN fonds fr. 12326 f. 79), quoted by Bennett, *Rediscovery*, p. 128. An edition is promised by D. Crahay in *Speculum* 38 (1984), pp. 319–22, fn. 2.

87 Amiens, Bibl. municipale, fonds L'Escalopier 94, written in 1461.

88 De Poerck 1961, p. 32. Bennett, *Rediscovery*, pp. 112–22.

89 Mourin 1955 and Goosse 1960.

90 De Poerck 1961, p. 38 dissents.

91 Goosse 1960, p. 85.

92 Bennett, *Rediscovery*, p. 113, n. 6.

to see why d'Outremeuse would there attribute to 'Mandeville' a Latin lapidary if the French lapidary were already in existence. On balance, it would appear that the idea of the lapidary and then of the 'collected works' mark the fourth and fifth stages in the development of the legend of the Liège connection with 'Mandeville', after the emergence of the Liège Version *c.* 1373, the Latin translation *c.* 1376, and the *Tresorier*. Such vigorous growth within twenty-five years is almost evangelical. If d'Outremeuse were not the prime instigator of each stage of this growth, there must have existed at Liège a very active and well co-ordinated 'Mandeville' industry during the last quarter of the fourteenth century.[93]

The epitaph

The most immediate result of d'Outremeuse's fictions was the setting up of an epitaph where the real Jean de Bourgogne had been buried in 1372 in the church of the Guillelmins, an order of hermits founded by William de Maleval (d. 1157) and later absorbed into the Augustinians; the Liège house existed from 1287 until the Revolution. Neither the date nor the author of the epitaph is known; possibly d'Outremeuse himself as the real or *soi-disant* executor of Bourgogne was responsible. It is first recorded in 1462 by Jacob Püterich von Reicherthausen:

> Hic iacet nobilis Dominus Joannes de Montevilla Miles, alias dictus ad Barbam, Dominus de Compredi, natus de Anglia, medicinae professor et devotissimus orator et bonorum suorum largissimus pauperibus erogator qui totam orbem peragravit in stratu Leodii diem vitae sua clausit extremum. Anno domini millesimo trecentesimo septuagesimo secundo mensis Februarii septimo.[94]

It was again reported by Abraham Ortelius in 1575, with some variations which suggest that he saw a later tombstone with a more polished latinity:

> 1 Montevilla]Mandeville   2 Compredi]Campdi   3 suorum]*omits*   3–4 totam ... stratu]toto quasi urbe lustrato   5 secundo ... septimo]uno novembris die xvii.

This later reading, which accords more closely with the details found in *Ly myreur des histors*, was confirmed by Rev. Edmund Lewknor before 1619, John Weever 1631, Rev. Charles Ellis 1699, and Pierre Lambinet 1799, except that all four gave the date of death as 1372.[95]

---

93 Cf. the contemporary industry of MM. De Poerck, Goosse, Mourin, and their pupils and confrères, in Belgium.

94 Hamelius ed., *op. cit.*, II. 1.

95 Reported by Bennett, *Rediscovery*, p. 90 and R. Lejeune p. 421.

The epitaph was accompanied by an engraved device. Von Reicherthausen reported a roaring lion with a forked tail being triumphed by an armed knight.[96] Ortelius reported a similar engraving, adding that the knight's shield, worn bare in his time, had once, by report, contained a lion *argent* with crescent *gules* on an *azure* ground with bordure indented *or*.[97] This device resembles the arms of the Montfort family: *gules*, a lion rampant tail fourchee *argent*,[98] with differences which may or may not be intentional; and supports the fiction that 'Mandeville' was a member of that family. The absence of the title *comte de Montfort* from the epitaph is interesting . Since the story of the identity of 'Mandeville' and de Bourgogne always contained the Montfort fiction, its expression in a device but not in words may reflect a later prudence. The tomb was certainly held to be that of Sir John Mandeville.

This certainty is shown in a reference by the *curé* de Saint André to a house in la rue de la Wache in 1459

la Mandeveles ly chevalier d'Engleterre qui avoit esteit par universe monde soloit demoureir, ki gist a Wilemiens,[99]

which had in 1388 been described as the lodging of 'maistre Johan alle Barbe'.[100] And it is reflected by the chronicler Raoul de Rivo (d. 1403) who wrote *sub anno* 1367:

Ioannes Mandevilius natione Anglus vir ingenio et arte medendi eminens, qui toto fere terrarum orbe peregrato, tribus linguis peregrinationem suam doctissime conscripsit, in alium orbem nullis finibus clausum, longeque hoc quietiorem, et beatiorem migravit 17 Novembris. Sepultus in Ecclesia Wilhelmitarum non procul a moenibus Civitatis Leodiensis.[101]

This notice, with its false date of 1367 and its false claim that 'Mandeville' wrote in *tribus linguis* (presumably the Liège Version, its Latin translation, and its German translation by Otto von Diemeringen, d. 1398), may not

96 Bennett, *Rediscovery*, pp. 100–2.

97 *Ibid.* 98 *Ibid.*

99 Item ly luminaire de St Gengul x. sous bon que Iohan Spiroule le pottir de staen solloit payer gisan sour une manson a piet delle Pond' Ile la Mandavele ly chevalier d Engleterre quy mort esteit par universe monde solloit demoreir ki gist a Willmins et est mentenant appartenans a Iohan: Registre aux Cens et Rentes de St André et de St Gengul, f. 8, Archives de St Antoine, reported by T. Gobert, *Liège à travers les âges* (1926) IV. 43, 46 and E. Poncelet, 'Les domaines urbains de Liège' in *Documents et Mémoires sur le Pays de Liège* (1947), p. 190. Cf. De Poerck 1961, p. 40, n. 4. A further reference to 'Mandavele' as living in a house on the corner of la rue de la Wache and la rue de l'église St Gangulphe occurs in a rent list for repair of fabric of the church dated 1459, reported by Gobert, *loc. cit.*

100 Relevat le dit Ottelet de This de Viller par le reportation Raskin le Cornus et fut iadis Mestre Iohan ale barbe: Archives de l'abbaye de Val Benoît, document dated 1386, reported by Gobert and Poncelet, *loc. cit.*

101 Hamelius ed., *op. cit.*, II. 3 and R. Lejeune p. 414.

depend on a personal knowledge of the epitaph but it clearly derives in some
way from it.

Similar notices, with the correct date 1372, are reported by Cornelius
Zanfliet at Liège *c.* 1460, Riccobald of Ferrara in 1474, Hartmann Schedel
in 1493, and several others, including Leland and Bale, in the sixteenth
century.[102] With the possible exception of Zanfliet, none is of independent
value.

Later accretions

Louis Abry, a Liège herald (d. 1720), claimed that Mandeville, otherwise Jean
de Bourgogne, left to the church of the Guillelmins several manuscripts of
his works, both *Voyages* and medical writings, written in his own hand.[103]
This appears to be an embellishment of d'Outremeuse's claim to have been
the executor of 'Mandeville'. If the brothers acquired copies of such works
(which is entirely possible, given the interest in the tombstone), none sur-
vives. Subsequently, a bibliographical confusion made by Fabricius in 1736,
between Mandeville and John Manduith, a fellow of Merton College (*fl.*
1340), led to three of the latter's works being credited to 'Mandeville',
Tabula astronomicae, De chorda recta, and *De doctrina theologica.*[104]

More exotically, a forged letter purporting to come from 'Mandeville'
himself and written in the fifteenth century, accompanied the acquisition of
a Latin manuscript of *Mandeville's Travels* and a piece of wood, presumably *lignum aloes,* which came from a river of Paradise, and other items by
the Benedictine cathedral priory of Christ Church at Canterbury.[105] The
miraculously preserved apple, encased in a crystal orb, which was shown to
Leland as a gift from 'Sir John Mandeville' when he visited Becket's shrine
was presumably part of this donation.[106]

Likewise, the Benedictine abbey of St Albans, where an English manuscript of *Mandeville's Travels* (now MS. Egerton 1982) passed to Caxton in
1490, set up an effigy of 'Mandeville' in armour, which was seen by Norden
in 1599, and later a commemorative plaque with attendant verses, which was
seen by Weever in 1631, who also reports that 'his kniues, the furniture of
his horse, and his spurres' were on display.[107]

102 Hamelius, *loc. cit.* and R. Lejeune p. 420.
103 Bennett, *Rediscovery,* p. 154, following Bormann; see note 78 above.
104 *Ibid.,* p. 155.
105 Seymour, *NQ* (1974).
106 J. Leland, *Comm. de scriptoribus,* ed. A. Hall (1709) I. 368.
107 Bennett, *Rediscovery,* p. 213. None of this is recorded in the inventory of 1428 printed
in *Chronica monasterii s. Albani,* ed. H.T. Riley, Rolls series.

In 1746 William Thompson wrote in his very defective English manuscript of *Mandeville's Travels* (now Bodleian Library MS. Douce 109): 'I had the Book from a Descendant by the Mother's Side from Sir John Mandeville', a claim repeated by Francis Douce (d. 1834) in another manuscript (now British Library MS. Additional 33758).[108] This claim, if not wholly the invention of a fraudulent bookseller, may be linked to the tradition that Sir John Mandeville, rector of Burnham Thorpe, Norfolk (1427–41), was the continuator of the *Brut* chronicle.[109]

The chronology of the myth

A chronology of the successive stages in the fabrication of the Liège myth makes clear, in classic example, how a legend is created.

1356 the author of *Mandeville's Travels* claims that he is Sir John Mandeville, born and bred at St Albans

1372 death of Jean de Bourgogne *à la barbe*, a physician and author of a plague tract, at Liège and burial at the Guillemins

c. 1373 the Liège Version states that the author wrote at Liège at the request of Jean de Bourgogne

1375 the Latin Vulgate translation of the Liège Version develops this claim, describing a meeting between the author and Jean de Bourgogne at the Caliph's court at Cairo

c. 1388 Jean d'Outremeuse in his *Myreur des histors* claims that on his deathbed Jean de Bourgogne revealed that he was Sir John Mandeville 'count of Montfort', who had lived in Liège since 1343, having fled England after unlawfully killing an unnamed adversary

before 1390 d'Outremeuse in his lapidary *Tresorier* cites Mandeville three times as one of his authorities and claims that he possesses the gems given to Mandeville during his sojourn at Alexandria

before 1400 four short tracts, allegedly written by Mandeville, appear as a supplement to *Mandeville's Travels* in Chantilly MS. 699

c. 1400 an epitaph at the Guillemins records the death of Sir John Mandeville *alias dictus ad Barbam* 7 February 1371 (*va.* 17 November 1371/2)

before 1403 the chronicler Raoul de Rivo reports that Mandeville died 17 November 1367 and was buried at the Guillemins

1459 a house in la rue de la Wache, described in 1388 as the lodging of *Maistre Johan alle Barbe*, is described as the former lodging of Mandeville.

108 Seymour, *Trans. Edinburgh* (1966), pp. 190–1.
109 *Ibid.*, p. 183.

BIBLIOGRAPHY

The manuscripts are listed in their three main traditions, and within each tradition are grouped according to version. Where the manuscript affiliation is known, the manuscripts of that version are listed by subgroups and closely affiliated manuscripts are bracketed together. Where the affiliations have still to be determined, the manuscripts are listed by their present or last known location. The listings depend in part on personal inspection, in part on catalogues and other publications, and notice of error and omission will be gratefully received. The British Library and la Bibliothèque Nationale are designated by their initials.

The editions are listed by language and identified by version. The English editions, which represent the dominant form of the book, are recorded in full. Editions in other languages, which have been less exhaustively studied, are generally reported only when they are incunables or modern editions. Pressmarks of copies of early material in the British Library, which holds the most complete (though not comprehensive) collection of editions of *Mandeville's Travels*, and in other libraries where the British Library lacks a copy are given.

The secondary sources list modern statements about the author and his book which are found in publications other than editions.

Scholars working on any aspect of *Mandeville's Travels* in any language who wish to contribute to and receive the annual Mandeville Newsletter are invited to write to the author of this monograph.

MANUSCRIPTS OF THE CONTINENTAL TRADITION

THE CONTINENTAL VERSION is the oldest French version and the nearest, within present knowledge, to the author's holograph. Classified by Schepens.

Subgroup A

1 Milan, Bibl. Trivulziana MS. 816 (dated 1396)
2 Rome, Bibl. Vaticana MS. Regina lat. 837
3 Paris, Bibl. de l'Arsenal MS. 3219
4 Paris, BN MS. MS. fonds fr. 25284 (conflated with Insular Version)
5 Paris, BN MS. fondation Smith-Lesouëf 65 (conflated with Insular Version)
6 Berne, Bürgerbibliothek MS. 125
7 Paris, BN MS. ancien fonds fr. 2129
8 Paris, BN MS. fonds fr. 5634
9 Paris, BN MS. nouv. acq. 4515 (dated 1371, printed by Letts)
10 Rome, Bibl. Vaticana MS. Regina lat. 750
11 Tours, Bibl. Municipale MS. 947
12 Modena, Bibl. Estense MS. fonds étranger 33 (dated 1388)
13 London, BL MS. Harley 3940
14 Paris, BN MS. fonds fr. 5637
15 Paris, BN MS. fonds fr. 6109

Subgroup B

16 Amiens, Bibl. Municipale MS. fonds l'Escalopier 95
17 Brussels, Bibl. Royale MS. 10439
18 Brussels, Bibl. Royale MS. 11141 (dated 1463)
19 Berne, Bürgerbibliothek MS. A 280
20 Brussels, Bibl. Royale MS. 14787
21 Dijon, Bibl. Municipale MS. ancien fonds 549
22 Cambridge, Mass., Harvard University MS. Riant 50
23 Paris, BN MS. nouv. acq. 10723
24 Brussels, Bibl. Royale MS. 10437–40, part 3
25 Paris, BN MS. fonds fr. 20145
26 Paris, BN MS. fonds fr. 1403
27 Lille, Bibl. Municipale MS. fonds Godefroy 121 (dated 1472)
28 Paris, BN MS. fonds fr. 5586 (dated 1477)

Unclassified

29 Cambridge, Fitzwilliam Museum MS. CFM 23
30 Sion, Bibl. Cantonale du Valais MS. Supersaxo 99
31 Phillipps MS. 1930 (present location unknown)

In addition, Aix, Bibl. Municipale MS. 437 is a 17c. copy of an early French print.

THE VELSER VERSION is a German translation of the Continental Version, subgroup A, made from a lost manuscript (close to Modena, Bibl. Estense MS. fonds ètranger 33 and its affiliates) by Michel Velser in 1393. Velser then made a second, abridged, and apparently revised translation, after reference to another manuscript of the Continental Version, before 1409. Described and classified by Morrall.

1st recension

32 Stuttgart, Württembergische Landesbibliothek HS. HB V 86 (dated 1472), printed
   by Morrall)
33 Donaueschingen, Fürstlich Fürstenbergische Hofbibliothek HS. 483 (dated 1435)
34 Basel, Universitätsbibliothek HS. E. IV. 1 (dated 1460)

Independently derived

35 Halle, Universitäts- und Landesbibliothek Sachsen-Anhalt HS. Yd 8. 4°

2nd recension, Subgroup A

36 Munich, Bayerische Staatsbibliothek HS. CGM 332 (dated 1409)
37 Wrocław, Biblioteka Uniwesytecka HS. M 1073 (dated 1414)
38 Vienna, Nationalbibliothek HS. 12. 475 (dated 1426)
39 Harburg, Bibliothek und Kunstsammlung, Fürstlich Oettingen-Wallerstein'sches
   Archiv HS. I. 3. fol. 11

2nd recension, Subgroup B

[40 Vienna, Nationalbibliothek HS. 2850
  41 St Paul in Kärnten, Stiftsbibliothek HS. 26. 4. 29
  42 Munich, Bayerische Staatsbibliothek HS. CGM 694
[43 Munich, Bayerische Staatsbibliothek HS. CGM 4872
  44 Göttingen, Universitätsbibliothek HS. Hist. 823 (dated 1470)
[45 Klosterneuburg, Stiftsbibliothek HS. 1083 (dated 1425)
  46 Munich, Universitätsbibliothek HS. 8° Cod MS 179 (dated 1434)
[47 Tambach, Gräflich Ortenburg'sche Bibliothek HS 7 (imperfect, dated 1444)
  48 Munich, Bayerische Staatsbibliothek HS. CGM 299
[49 Munich, Bayerische Staatsbibliothek HS. CGM 594
[50 Dresden, Sächsische Landesbibliothek HS. F 184b

51 Brňo, Universitní knihovna HS. Mk 84
52 Wolfenbüttel, Herzog August Bibliothek HS. Guelf 23. 10. Aug. 4° (dated 1436)
53 Munich, Bayerische Staatsbibliothek HS. CGM 695 (dated 1473)

2nd recension, Subgroup C

54 Giessen, Universitätsbibliothek HS. 992
55 Warsaw, Biblioteka Narodowa HS. 4352 (dated 1412)
56 Minneapolis, University of Minnesota MS. 18 (dated 1455)
57 Berlin. Staatsbibliothek HS. Germ. Fol. 1066
58 Heidelberg, Universitätsbibliothek HS. Pal. Germ. 806
59 Harburg, Fürstlich Oettingen-Wallerstein'sches Archiv HS. I. 3. 4°. 8
60 Munich, Bayerische Staatsbibliothek HS. CGM 252
61 Innsbruck, Universitätsbibliothek HS. 750
62 Salzburg, Benediktiner-Erzabtei St Peter MS. b. IV. 37
63 New York, Public Library MS. Spencer 37 (dated 1457)
64 Sion, Bibl. Cantonale du Valais MS. Supersaxo 94

2nd recension, Subgroup D

65 Munich, Bayerische Statsbibliothek HS. L 1603
66 London, BL MS. Additional 18026 (dated 1449)
67 Berlin, Staatsbibliothek HS. Germ. Fol. 1066 (dated 1462)
68 Bamburg, Staatliche Bibliothek HS. Msc hist 182 (dated 1475)
69 London, BL MS. Additional 10129

THE ITALIAN VERSION is a translation of the Continental Version made before 1432.

70 London, BL MS. Additional 41329 (dated 1469)
71 Oxford, Bodleian Library MS. Addition C 252 (dated 1442)
72 New York, Pierpont Morgan Library MS. M 746 (dated 1465)
73 Lawrence, University of Kansas Library MS. 16 (fragment, 20ff.)
74 Munich, Bayerische Staatsbibliothek MS. Ital. 1009
75 Florence, Biblioteca Nazionale Centrale MS. Magl. XXXV. 221 (printed by Zambrini)
76 Florence, Biblioteca Riccardiana MS. 1910 (16c.)
77 Florence, Biblioteca Riccardiana MS. 1917 (dated 1492)
78 Lucca, Biblioteca Governativa MS. 304 (16c.)
79 Mantua, Biblioteca Comunale MS. (dated 1432)
80 Milan, Biblioteca Ambrosiana MS. H 188 (dated 1478)
81 Naples, Biblioteca Nazionale MS. XII D 57 (dated 1467)
82 Parma, Biblioteca Palatina MS. 1070 (dated 1465)

In addition, Venice Biblioteca Marciana MS. It. VI 208 ff. 160–77 contains extracts from this version, dated 1518–20 and possibly taken from an early print.

THE SPANISH VERSION is a translation of the Continental Version made before 1395.

83 El Escorial, Biblioteca del Real Monasterio MS. M–iii-7 (printed by Montañés)

THE DUTCH VERSION is a translation of the Continental Version made before 1430. Described and classified by Ganser 1985.

Subgroup A

84 Berlin, Staatsbibliothek HS. Germ. Fol. 550
85 Berlin, Staatsbibliothek HS. Germ. Qu. 322
86 Cape Town, Public Library MS. Grey I

Subgroup B

87 The Hague, Koninklijke Bibliotheek MS. 131 B 14 (dated 1462)
88 Göttingen, Universitätsbibliothek HS. histor. 823 b
89 Berlin, Staatsbibliothek HS. Germ. Fol. 204
90 Lüneburg, Ratsbücherei HS. hist. c 2° 8

Subgroup C

91 Berlin, Staatsbibliothek HS. Germ. Qu. 271 (dated 1430)
92 Brussels, Bibl. Royale MS. 720–22
93 Leiden, Bibliotheek der Rijksuniversiteit MS. BPL 14 f. (ff. 1–13^r derive from Otto von Diermeringen's German translation)
94 Leiden, Bibliotheek der Rijksuniversiteit MS. BPL 1983
95 Marburg, Universitätsbibliothek HS. Mscr 76
96 Soest, Stadtbibliothek HS. Nr. 28 (dated 1490)
97 Düsseldorf, Universitätsbibliothek HS. K 20 (one leaf)

MANUSCRIPTS OF THE INSULAR TRADITION

THE INSULAR VERSION is a French recension, made in England before 1375, of the original French text. Classified by Seymour. The manuscripts of subgroup C derive from a common ancestor (copied from a lost manuscript of subgroup B) which was taken from England to France before 1402 and were all written in France, and occasionally there conflated with manuscripts of the Continental Version.

Subgroup A

1 London, BL MS. Harley 204
2 London, BL MS. Harley 212
3 London, BL MS. Harley 1739
4 London, BL MS. Harley 4383 (printed by Warner)
5 London, BL MS. Royal 20 A. i
6 London, BL MS. Royal 20 B. x (printed in part by Warner)
7 Oxford, Bodleian Library MS. Bodley 841
8 Oxford, Bodleian Library MS. Asmole 1804
9 Durham, Cathedral Library MS. B. iii. 3
10 New York, Pierpont Morgan Library MS. M 957

Subgroup B

11 Oxford, Bodleian Library, MS. Additional C 280
12 London, BL MS. Sloane 1464 (collated by Warner)
13 London, BL. MS. Sloane 560
14 Leiden, Bibliotheek der Rijksuniversiteit MS. Vossius Lat. F 75

Subgroup C

15 London, BL MS. Additional 33757 (collated by Warner)
16 Cambridge, Fitzwilliam Museum MS. CFM 23
17 Durham, University Library MS. Cosin V. i. 10
18 Bern, Bürgerbibliothek MS. 58
19 Lyon, Palais des Arts MS. 28
20 Paris, BN MS. fonds fr. 5633
21 Paris, BN MS. fonds fr. 25284
22 Paris, BN MS. fonds fr. 5635
23 Paris, BN MS. ancien fonds fr. 2810

In addition, two loose leaves of this version (present whereabouts unknown) are reported in a letter of the late 19c. kept with Yale University MS 86, which quotes a passage beginning *estre appelle Collos* (i.e. Warner's edition p.13, line 39); cf. Phillipps MS. 4439 (sold Sotheby's 11 June 1898, lot 967; present whereabouts unknown), a copy of a *Regula sacodotum*, which contains at its end two leaves of a French version of Mandeville.

THE ROYAL VERSION is a Latin translation of the Insular Version subgroup A, most closely related to MS. Royal 20 A. i.

24 London, BL MS. Royal 13 E. ix (printed in part by Seymour 1963)
25 London, BL MS. Harley 175
26 London, BL MS. Cotton Appendix iv
27 Glasgow, Hunterian Museum MS. T. 4. 1
28 Cambridge, Jesus College MS. Q. B. 18
29 Durham, University Library MS. Cosin V. iii. 7
30 London, BL MS. Cotton Otho D. i (an epitome)

THE LEIDEN VERSION is a Latin translation, made before 1390, of the Insular Version, subgroup B, most closely related to BL MS. Sloane 560.

32 Leiden, Bibliotheek der Rijksuniversiteit MS. Vulcan 96
32 Cambridge, Corpus Christi College MS. 275
33 London, BL MS. Egerton 672
34 Cambridge, Corpus Christi College MS. 426, part II (extracts)
    Cardiff, Public Library MS. 3. 236 (final two leaves only)

THE HARLEY VERSION is a Latin translation of the Insular Version, subgroup B.

35 London, BL MS. Harley 82 (printed in part by Seymour 1973)

THE ASHMOLE VERSION is a Latin translation of the Insular Version, subgroup B.

36 Oxford, Bodleian Library, MS. Ashmole 769

THE DEFECTIVE VERSION is an English translation of the Insular Version, subgroup B, from a lost manuscript which lacked its second quire. Described and classified by Seymour 1966.

Subgroup A

37 Corning N.Y., Corning Museum of Glass MS. 6
38 Cambridge, Magdalene College MS. Pepys 1955 (ff. 1–6 printed by Doyle and
    Seymour)

39 Cambridge, University Library MS. Dd. i. 17
40 Oxford, Balliol College MS. 239
41 Oxford, The Queen's College MS. 383
42 Oxford, Bodleian Library MS. Rawlinson D 101
43 Oxford, Bodleian Library MS. Douce 33
44 Bodleian Library MS. Ashmole 751 (extracts, printed by Seymour 1961)
45 Cambridge, University Library MS. Ff. v. 35
46 Oxford, Bodleian Library MS. e Musæo 124

Subgroup B

47 London, BL MS. Arundel 140
48 London, BL MS. Royal 17 B. xliii
49 London, BL MS. Harley 2386
50 London, BL MS. Harley 3954
51 San Marino, Calif., Huntington Library MS. HM 114

Independently derived

52 London, BL MS. Royal 17 C. xxxviii

Subgroup C

53 Rugby School MS. Bloxam 1008
54 London, BL MS. Additional 33758
55 Cambridge, Trinity College MS. R. 4. 20
56 Oxford, Bodleian Library MS. Douce 109
57 Oxford, Bodleian Library MS. Rawlinson B 216
58 Oxford, Bodleian Library MS. Rawlinson D 100
59 Oxford, Bodleian Library MS. Lat. misc. e 85 (chapters 13–15 only)
60 The Sneyd Manuscript (bought by Maggs at Sotheby S.C. October 1945 item
      2023, present whereabouts unknown)
61 Cambridge, Fitzwilliam Museum MS. Bradfer-Lawrence Dep BL7

Subgroup D

62 Cambridge, University Library MS. Gg. i. 34, part 3
63 Oxford, Bodleian Library MS. Additional C 285
64 Oxford, Bodleian Library MS. Tanner 405
65 Princeton, University Library MS. Taylor 10
66 Manchester, Chetham's Library MS. 6711

Subgroup E

67 Edinburgh, National Library of Scotland MS. Advocates 19. 1. 11
68 Dublin, Trinity College MS. E. 5. 6

69 Oxford, Bodleian Library MS. Rawlinson D 652
70 Oxford, Bodleian Library MS. Laud Misc. 699
71 London, BL MS. Sloane 2319
72 London, BL MS. Additional 37049 (an epitome, printed by Seymour 1966)

In addition there are brief extracts (printed by Horner) in Oxford, Bodleian Library MS. Digby 88 f. 28 and two discontinuous leaves from Chapters 6 and 9 (printed by Cawley) in a printed book, *Petri Carpentarii... Epistola* in the Library of Ripon Cathedral. Latin extracts of letters taken from a manuscript of subgroup E occur in Bodleian Library MS. Douce 45 ff. 118–20.

THE COTTON VERSION is a conflation in English based on the Defective Version, subgroup A and expanded by reference to the Insular Version, subgroup A.

73 London, BL MS. Cotton Titus C. xvi (printed by Seymour 1967)

THE EGERTON VERSION is a conflation in English based on the Defective Version, subgroup A, and a lost English translation of the Royal Version, with reference to an Insular manuscript.

74 London, BL MS. Egerton 1982 (printed by Warner)

THE BODLEY VERSION is an abridgement of the lost English translation of the Royal Version.

75 Oxford, Bodleian Library MS. Rawlinson D 99 (printed by Letts)
76 Oxford, Bodleian Library MS. e Musæo 116 (printed by Seymour 1963)

THE METRICAL VERSION is an English rendering in couplets of the text close to the Harley translation of the Insular Version, subgroup B.

77 Coventry, City Record Office MS. (printed by Seymour 1973)

THE STANZAIC FRAGMENT is an English verse rendering of parts of Chapters 15 and 23, possibly based on the Cotton Version, with parts of Marco Polo (in Pipino's version).

78 Oxford, Bodleian Library MS. e Musæo 160 (printed by Seymour 1964b)

THE IRISH VERSION was translated from the Defective Version, subgroup A, in 1475 by Finghin Ó Mathghamhna.

79 London, BL MS. Egerton 1781 (edited by Gleeson).
80 Rennes, Bibl. Muncipale MS. 598 (printed by Stokes)
81 London, BL MS. Additional 33993 (extracts, printed by Doyle and Seymour)

MANUSCRIPTS OF THE LIÈGE TRADITION

THE LIÈGE VERSION is a French recension of the Continental Version, made at Liège *c.* 1373 and including references to Ogier le Danois.

1 Madrid, Bibl. Nacional MS. 9602
2 Brussèls, Bibl. Royale MS. 10420–25
3 Paris, BN MS. fonds fr. 14436 (dated 1396)
4 Amiens, Bibl. Municipale MS. fonds l'Escalopier 94 (dated 1461)
5 Chantilly, Musée Condé MS. 699
6 Grenoble, Bibl. Municipale MS. 962
7 Cambridge, Fitzwilliam Museum MS. McClean 177

THE LATIN VULGATE VERSION is a Latin translation of the Liège Version made in 1375 and mainly extant in Central European hands.

England

8 London, BL MS. Harley 3589
9 London, BL MS. Additional 37512 (dated 1457)
10 Oxford, Bodleian Library MS. Fairfax 23
11 Oxford, Bodleian Library MS. Addition A 187 (dated 1445)
12 Oxford, Bodleian Library MS. Laud Misc. 721 (dated 1454)

France

13 Paris, BN MS. Lat 6447
14 Strasbourg, Bibl. Universitaire et Régionale MS. 30
15 Charleville, Bibl. Municipale MS. 62

Belgium

16 Brussels, Bibl. Royale MS. 21520
17 Brussels, Bibl. Royale MS. 1160–63
18 Liège, Bibl. de l'Université MS. 354 (dated 1458)
19 Liège, Bibl. de l'Université MS. Wittert 99

Italy

20 Turin, Bibl. Nazionale MS. H. III. 1

21 Belluno, Bibl. Lolliniana MS. 39
22 Rome, Bibl. Vaticana MS. Fondo Chigi F VII 171

USA

23 New York, Columbia University MS. Plimpton 264 (dated 1456)
24 Lawrence, University of Kansas MS. 19
25 Minneapolis, University of Minnesota MS. 3 (dated 1433)
26 Minneapolis, University of Minnesota MS. 13, part I
27 Minneapolis, University of Minnesota MS. 13, part II

Austria

28 Klosterneuburg, Stiftsbibliothek HS. Can. Reg. 132 (dated 1452)
29 Vienna, Nationalbibliothek HS. 43/265 (dated 1445)
30 Vienna, Nationalbibliothek HS. 4449, item 15 ff. 112–31
31 Vienna, Nationalbibliothek HS. 5363

Denmark

32 Copenhagen, Kongelige Bibliotek HS. S 445 (dated 1434)

Germany

33 Berlin, Staatsbibliothek HS. Lat. Qu. 711
34 Berlin, Staatsbibliothek HS. Diez C Fol. (dated 1445)
35 Berlin, Staatsbibliothek HS. Lat. Fol. 179
36 Gotha, Herzogliche Bibliothek HS. 192
37 Düsseldorf, Universitätsbibliothek HS. G12
38 Giessen, Universitätsbibliothek HS. 140
39 Hamburg, Stadtbibliothek HS. Hist. 31b
40 Harburg, Bibliothek und Kunstsammlung, Fürstlich Oettingen-Wallerstein' sches
    Archiv HS. 1, 2, fol, 31
41 Wolfenbüttel, Herzog August Bibliothek HS. 3137, item 18 (dated 1474)
42 Wolfenbüttel, Herzog August Bibliothek HS. 3266 (dated 1461)
43 Gotha, Forschungsbibliothek HS. 192

Czechoslovakia

44 Brňo, Státní Universitní MS. Mk 29

In addition, Göttingen, Universitätsbibliothek HS. Hist. 61 ff. 1–79 gives a mixed
Latin and German text of this version. A manuscript from the Abbaye de St Jacques
at Liège, sold at auction at Liège 3 March 1788, is apparently lost. The manuscript
of the version reported by Vogels, *Lateinischen Versionen* p. 7 as Stadtbibliothek
Trier HS. 334 is not in that library. HS. 334, item 7 (ff. 135–43) of the

48 BIBLIOGRAPHY

Universitätsbibliothek von Königsburg (now Kaliningrad, Russia), a fragment imperfect at beginning and end, was apparently destroyed with the university in 1944. London, BL MS. Additional 24189, which contains 28 pictures illustrating the first five chapters of Mandeville (possibly a fragment of a larger volume), was probably based on a copy of the Latin Vulgate Version written in Bohemia, not on the Czech translation as some claim; see M. Štefanová in *Umení* 33 (1985) 315–29 and D. Heydová in *Umení* 35 (1987) 507–14.

THE DIEMERINGEN VERSION is a German translation of the Latin Vulgate Version made by Otto von Diemeringen in 1398.

45 Paris, BN MS. allemand 150 (dated 1418)
46 Sélestat, Bibl. Municipale MS. 25 (dated 1421)
47 Strasbourg, Bibl. Universitaire et Régionale MS. 2119
48 London, BL MS. Additional 17335
49 St Gall, Stiftsbibliothek HS. 628
50 Vienna, Nationalbibliothek HS. 2828 (dated 1476)
51 Vienna, Nationalbibliothek HS. 12449
52 Lawrence, University of Kansas MS. 18
53 Lawrence, University of Kansa MS. 17 (fragment, 18ff.)

Germany

54 Bamberg, Staatliche Bibliothek HS. Misc. hist. J.H.112
55 Berlin, Staatsbibliothek HS. Germ. Fol. 206
56 Berlin, Staatsbibliothek HS. Germ. Fol. 1268
57 Coburg, Bibl. des Gymnasium Casimirianum HS. Sche 16, item 5
58 Erlangen, Universitätsbibliothek HS. 2112, item 35
59 Heidelberg, Universitätsbibliothek HS. Pal. Germ. 65
60 Heidelberg, Universitätsbibliothek HS. Pal. Germ. 138
61 Karlsruhe, Badische Landesbibliothek HS. 167 (dated 1416)
62 Munich, Bayerische Staatsbibliothek HS. CGM 329
63 Munich, Bayerische Statsbibliothek HS. 593
64 Munich, Bayerische Staatsbibliothek HS. 693 (dated 1459)
65 Wiesbaden, Staatsarchiv HS. B 25
66 Wolfenbüttel, Braunschweigische Landesbibliothek HS. 14. 10 Aug (dated 1473)
67 Wolfenbüttel, Braunschweigische Landesbibliothek HS. 32. 8 Aug
68 Würzburg, Universitätsbibliothek HS. Fol. 38 (before 1464)
69 Gotha, Forschungsbibliothek HS. A 26 (dated 1472)
70 Gotha, Forschungsbibliothek HS. 584

In addition, one manuscript of the former Fürstlich Lobkowitzsche Bibliothek, Prague (HS 421) is unlocated. The manuscript of the version reported by Schoerner no. 24 as Stadtbibliothek Trier HS. 1935 ff. 122–199 is not in that library. Three manuscripts of this version appear in a Low German dialect:

71 Hamburg, Staats- und Universitätsbibliothek HS. Geog. 58 (dated 1447)
72 Magdeburg, Stadsbibliothek HS. XII. 15 (dated 1420)
73 Lüneburg, Ratsbücherei HS. D. 25 (very imperfect)

A brief extract in a Low German dialect, extant in Uppsala University Library MS. C. 360 ff. 110ᵛ–6ᵛ, is printed by M. Andersson-Schmitt in *Niederdeutsches Jahrbuch* III (1988) 53–62.

THE CZECH VERSION was translated from the German version of Otto von Diemeringen by Vivřincem Vavřinec before 1419.

74 Brňo, Universitní knihovna MS. Mk 80
75 Prague, Památník Národního Písemnictví MS. DF IV 43
76 Prague, Památník Národního Písemnictví MS. DG III 7 (dated 1449)
77 Prague, Narodni Museum MS. V E 11 (dated 1484)
78 Prague, Narodni Muzeum MS. III E 42
79 Prague, Královstvi Českého Muzeum MS. II. C 10, item 4 (ff. 157–225: dated 1445)
80 Prague, Královstvi Českého Muzeum MS. XXII. A4
81 Prague, Státní knihovna ČSR MS. 88 (dated 1472)

In addition there are three post-medieval manuscript copies of early prints and a small abstract.

THE DANISH VERSION was translated from the Latin Vulgate Version by Peder Hare in 1444. Three of the four manuscripts were written in the sixteenth century.

82 Stockholm, Kungliga Biblioteket MS. M306 (dated 1584)
83 Stockholm, Kungliga Biblioteket MS. M307 (dated 1459 and printed by Lorenzen)
84 Odense, Landsarkiv for Fyn, Karen Brahes MS. E III 6
85 Copenhagen, Kongelige Bibliotek MS. GKS 3559 (an epitome, 18 ff.)

EDITIONS

ENGLISH EDITIONS. Since 1499 these editions, all printed in Black Letter until 1696, have generally contained woodcuts. They are here listed with the names of their printers, all of London or Westminster unless otherwise stated. Pressmarks for British Library copies and for very early material in other libraries are given.

Incunables and early editions

[?1496] Richard Pynson, 72 pp. Unique copy in B.L. [G.6713], imperfect. One leaf in Bodley [Arch. G d. 31 (1)].

1499 Wynkyn De Worde, 112 pp. Imperfect copy in the Cambridge University Library [Inc 5.J.1.2].

1503 Wynkyn De Worde, 112 pp. Imperfect copies and substantial fragment in Bodley [Arch, A e 89 and Douce frag. e.8] and at Stonyhurst College, Whalley, Lancashire.

{?1510} Wynkyn De Worde. Two leaves in Bodley [Arch. G d. 31 (2)], one leaf in B.L. [Harley 5919, item 16].

1568 Thomas East, 94 pp. Copy in B.L. [1045 h.2]. Reprinted in a limited edition of 350 copies by the O.U.P. in 1932.

1582 Thomas East, 80 pp. Copies in Bodley [Douce MM 489] and the Folger Shakespeare Library.

Seventeenth century

1612 Thomas Snodham, 80 pp. Unique copy in the Library of Congress.

1618 Thomas Snodham, 80 pp. Copy in B.L. [G.6715].

1625 Thomas Snodham, 80 pp. Copies in the Folger Shakespeare Library, Huntington Library and at Chatsworth House.

1632 William Stansby. Copies in B.M. [G6714] and Yale University Library [Ecd 322 gk].

[1640] Richard Bishop. Copies in the Folger Shakespeare Library and Huntington Library.

1650 Richard Bishop. 'R.B. for E. Dod & N. Ekins'. Copy in John Rylands Library.

1657 Richard Bishop. 'Printed by R.B. and are to sold by *Andrew Crooke*, at the *Green Dragon* in S. Pauls Churchyard 1657'. Copy in B.L. [G.6716].

1670 'Printed for *Andrew Crooke*, 1670'. Copy in B.L. [10055 a.6].

1677 'Printed for *R. Scott, T. Basset, J. Wright and R. Chiswel*, 1677'. Copies in B.L. [C.32.d.42], Huntington Library, etc.

1677 'Printed for B. Tooke at the Ship in S. Pauls Churchyard; 1677'. Identical with the previous copy apart from head-name.

1684 'Printed for *R. Scott, T. Basset, J. Wright and R. Chiswel*, 1684'. Copies in B.L. [G6717 and 1045 h.30].

1696 'Printed for *Rich. Chiswell, B. Walford, Mat. Wotton, and Geo. Conyers*, 1696'. Copy in B.L. [G.6718].

Eighteenth century

1704 Richard Chiswell.

1705 Richard Chiswell. Copy in B.L. [1077 g 35 (2)].

1722 'Printed by A. Wilde, for G. Conyers, in *Little-Britain*, T. Norris, at *London Bridge*, and A. Bettesworth in *Paternoster Row*'. Copy in B.L. [10056 c.22].

1725 'Printed for J. Woodman and D. Lyon and C. Davis'. The first modern edition, transcribed directly from the Cotton manuscript.

1727 Reprint of 1725 edition.

1730 'Printed for J. Osborne near Dock Head, Southwark and J. Hodges at the Looking Glass on London Bridge'. Reprints Wilde's text of 1722. Copies in B.L. [G.2247 and 10055 a. 33].

1745 'Printed for J. Hodges, at the Looking Glass opposite to St Magnut's Church, London Bridge, and J. Harris, the Looking Glass and Bible, on London Bridge'. Reprint of the previous edition. Copy in B.L. [435 a. 1].

1750 'Printed and sold in Aldermary Church Yard'. A chapbook of 24 pp. Copy in B.L. [1079 i.14 (23)]. Reprinted by J. Ashton, *Chap Books of the Eighteenth Century* (1882), pp 405–16.

1780 Reprint of 1750 chap book. Copy in B.L. [12315.aaa 6 (3)].

1785 Reprint of 1750 chap book. Copy in B.L. [1076 1.3 (12)].

n.d. Another reprint, Newcastle-upon-Tyne.

n.d. Another reprint, Bow Church Yard.

Nineteenth century

1839 Edward Lumley. Reprint of 1725 edition, with some editorial additions by J.O. Halliwell.

1848 Bohn's Antiquarian Library. *Early Travels in Palestine*, edited by T. Wright. Modernized text of 1725 edition.

1866 F.S. Ellis. Reprint of 1839 edition.

1869 Weidmannsche Buchhandlung. *Altenglische Sprachproben*, edited by E. Mätzner. Abridgement of 1839 edition, with notes.

1875 W.P. Nimmo. *The English Explorers*, edited by R. Cochrane. Copy in B.L. [10027.aaa].

1883 Reeves and Turner. Reprint of 1839 edition.

1886 Cassell & Co. Wright's text of 1848. Reprinted 1894, 1899, 1905, 1909.

1886 The Seaside Library, New York. Modernized edition by G. Munro.

1887 Pickering and Chatto. Reprint of East's text of 1568, with editorial additions
     by J. Ashton.
1889 The Roxburghe Club. A scholarly edition of the Egerton manuscript by G.F.
     Warner, with a French manuscript.
1892 E. Maynard & Co., New York. Reprint of Mätzner's abridged edition of 1869.
1895 Constable & Co. Modernized version of 1725, with some reference to the 1839
     edition, and with illustrations by A. Layard.
1898 D. Appleton & Co. Edited A. Layard and J.W. Redway. New York.

Twentieth century

1900 Macmillan & Co. Modernized text of the Cotton manuscript, edited by A.W.
     Pollard. Reprinted 1905, 1909, 1915, 1923, and in paperback in 1964 with
     reproductions of Anton Sorg's woodcuts of the 1481 Augsburg edition.
1905 F.S. Ellis. Reprint of 1866 edition.
1919 Early English Text Society. An edition of the Cotton manuscript by P.
     Hamelius. 2 vols.
1928 Grabhorn Press, San Francisco, for Random House, New York. A reprint,
     limited to 150 copies, of the 1725 text in fine binding.
1928 J.M. Dent & Sons. Everyman's Library edition by J. Bramont, based on East's
     text of 1568 with additions from the 1725 edition.
1932 H. Milford, for the Oxford University Press. A limited reprint of 350 copies
     of East's 1568 edition.
1953 The Hakluyt Society. Modernized text of the Egerton manuscript, with appa-
     ratus and transcriptions of a Bodley manuscript and an early French manu-
     script, by M. Letts.
1959 'The Defective Version of *Mandeville's Travels*', ed. M.C. Seymour. D. Phil.
     thesis, Oxford, vol. 2.
1963 Early English Text Society. An edition of a Bodley manuscript, with a Latin
     manuscript, by M.C. Seymour.
1967 The Clarendon Press. An edition of the Cotton manuscript with apparatus by
     M.C. Seymour.
1968 Oxford University Press. World's Classics edition with modernized spelling
     based on the 1967 text.
1973 Wm. Collins Sons & Co. An abridged edition, based on Pollard's text of 1900,
     by N. Denny and J. Filmer-Sankey.
1973 Early English Text Society. An edition of the Metrical Version, with a Latin
     manuscript, by M.C. Seymour.
n.d. Heron Books. A reprint of the Everyman's Library edition of 1928.
1980 Exeter University Press. A facsimile of the Pynson incunable, with introduc-
     tion by M.C. Seymour.
1983 Penguin Books. A modernized and bastardized edition of the Egerton manu-
     script, by C.W.R.D. Moseley.

LATIN EDITIONS. All editions apart from the two most recent are of the Vulgate Version. They are in two states, distinguished by the inclusion (in the Van Os and Leeu prints) or omission of references to Ogier le Danois.

1483 Pieter van Os. Zwolle. [Pierpont Morgan Library 32727]
[?1484] Printer of *Vitas Patrum* 1483. Strasbourg. [BL G 6700}
[1484] Gerard Leeu. Antwerp. [BL 566 f. 6]
1488 Cornelis de Zierikzee. Cologne. [BL G 6699]
1589 Richard Hakluyt. London.
1625 Samuel Purchas. London. An abridgement of Hakluyt's text.
1809 Rolls Series, *Hakluyt's Collections* II. 79–138. London. A reprint of the 1589 text.
1963 Early English Text Society. A partial edition of the Royal Version, by M.C. Seymour. A complete edition is given in his D. Phil. thesis, Oxford 1959, vol. 4.
1973 Early English Text Society. A partial edition of the Harley Version, by M.C. Seymour.
1983 George Braziller. New York. A facsimile of BL MS. Additional 24189, containing 28 illustrations of the first five chapters of the Vulgate Version, with introduction by J. Krássa (trans. P. Kussi).

FRENCH EDITIONS. There are six incunable editions and six editions of 16c. (1508, 1516, 1521, 1525, 1542, 1560: mostly printed at Lyon and with woodcuts in the Sorg tradition). All editions are of the Continental Version unless otherwise stated.

1480 Martin Hus. Lyon. [BN 2633]
1480 Guillaume le Roy. Lyon. [BL G 6775]
1483 Nicolaus Philippi et Marcus Reinhart. Lyon. 86 woodcuts, made from the blocks used in Sorg's 1481 German edition Woodcuts. [University of Liège C 66]
1487 Nicolaus Philippi et Jean du Pré. Lyon. Woodcuts.
1487 Jean Crés. Lantanec. [BN Res. O^2 f. 4]
1490 Pierre Bouttlelier. Lyon. Woodcuts. [Pierpont Morgan Library 610]
1508 Claude Nourry dit le Prince. Lyon.
1516 Barabe Chaussard. Lyon.
1521 Le Veufue feu Jehan Trepperel. Paris.
1525 Philippe le Noir. Paris.
1542 Jehan Canterel dit Motin. Lyon.
1560 Jehan Bonfons. Paris.
1729 *Recueil de divers Voyages curieux* II. 1–25, ed. P. Van Der Aa. Leiden. A French translation of the Latin abridgement by Purchas, London 1625.
1735 *Voyages faits principalement en Asie* I. 1–25, ed. P. Bergeron. The Hague. A reprint of the 1729 text.

1889 *The Buke of John Maundeuill... with the French text*, ed. G.F. Warner. West-
     minster. An edition of the Insular Version. Roxburghe Club.
1953 *Mandeville's Travels* II. 229–413, ed. M. Letts. An edition of the manuscript
     dated 1371 of the Continental Version. Hakluyt Society.

GERMAN EDITIONS. There are eight incunable editions and four editions in the
16c. (1501, 1507, 1580, and 1584 in *Reyssbuch dess heligen Lands* pp. 405–32); see
*Verzeichnis der im deutschen Sprachbereich erschienenen Druke des XVI.
Jahrhunderts* vol. X (1987) 171. Thereafter, there are several editions, often in larger
collections like the *Reyssbuch*, reprinted nine times, before 1900. Unless otherwise
stated here, all editions give the translation of Otto von Diemeringen, but Anton
Sorg's woodcuts and their derivatives are commonly found in all editions.

1478 Anton Sorg. Augsburg. Velser's translation. [fragment at Munich, Bayerische
     Staatsbibliothek]
1481 Anton Sorg. Augsburg. Velser's translation.
1482 Bernhard Richel. Basel.
1482 Johannes Schönsperger. Augsburg. Velser's translation. [BL 6774]
1483 Johannes Prüss. Strasbourg.
1484 Johannes Prüss. Strasbourg. [BL G 6773]. Reprinted in *Die deutschen
     Volksbücker*, item 51, Frankfurt-am-Main 1850–67.
1488 Johannes Prüss. Strasbourg.
1499 Bartholomaeus Kistler. Strasbourg. Reprinted Matthias Hüffus, Strasbourg 1856.
1965 'Otto von Diemeringen. A German Version of *Mandeville's Travels*', ed. E.W.
     Crosby. Ph.D. Kansas: DAI 27. 743A. An edition of the Univ. of Kansas
     manuscript.
1966 *Die Reisen des Ritters John Mandeveille*, ed. T. Stemmler. Stuttgart. A mod-
     ernized and bastardized edition, with woodcuts based on those of the 1499
     edition.
1974 *Sir John Mandevilles Reisebeschreibung*, ed. E.J. Morrall. A critical edition of
     Velser's translation.
1987 *Jean de Mandeville. Reisen*, ed. E. Bremer and K. Ridder, Leiden. A reprint
     of 1481 Sorg and 1482 Richel editions.
1989 *Das Reisebuch des Ritters John Mandeville*, ed. G.E. Sollbach. Frankfurt-am-
     Main. A modernized version of Schönsperger's 1482 edition.

IRISH EDITIONS. There are no early editions.

1898 W. Stokes, 'The Gaelic Mandeville', *Zeitschrift für celtische Philologie* II. 1–
     62, 226–312. An edition of the Rennes manuscript.
1961 T. Gleeson, 'The Irish Version of Mandeville'. MA thesis, University College,
     Cork. An edition of the Egerton manuscript.

ITALIAN EDITIONS. There are ten incunable editions and thirteen editions of 16c., mostly printed at Venice where there was a demand for information on routes to the eastern Mediterranean. Copies of the early editions are listed in *Indice Generale degli Incunaboli delle Biblioteche d'Italia* IV. 30–2, nos. 6098–109, and in *STC of books printed in Italy 1465–1600... British Museum* (1985) p. 408. See further A.L. Lepschy, 'Quel libro de Mandavilla... Italian incunables', in *Book Production and Letters... in honor of Conor Fahy*, ed. J. Took *et al.* (London 1986), pp. 209–19.

1480 Petri de Corneno. Milan. [BL G 6702]
1488 Ugo Rugerius. Bologna. [BL G 6703]. A second impression [BL IA 28809]
1491 Nicolo di Ferari. Venice. [BL G 6704]
1492 Lorenzo Morgiani e Johannes Petri da Maganza. Florence. [BL G 6705]
1492 Joanne Jacobo e Joanne Antonio di Beneditti. Bologna. [BL G 6706]
1496 Oldericho Scinzenzeler. Milan. [BL IA 26761]
1496 Manfredo da Moncrato da Streuo da Bonello. Venice. [BL G 6708]
1497 Piero e Jacobo da Campii. Bologna. [BL G 6110]
1497 Ulderico Scinzenzeler. Milan. [BL G 6709]. A second impression [BL IA 26788]
1870 F. Zambrini, *I Viaggi di Giovanni da Mandavilla*. 2 vols. Bologna. Reprinted in facsimile 1968, Bologna.
1982 *John Mandeville Viaggi*, ed. E. Barisone, Milan.

CZECH EDITIONS. Two early editions (1510 Pilsen, reprinted 1513) are now not known to be extant. Three later 16c. editions (1576 Prague, reprinted 1596, and 1600 Prague) are extant in PNP, Prague.

1796 Kramerius, Prague. Reprinted 1811. An edition of a lost manuscript dated 1687.
1911 F. Šimek, *Cestopis T. Zv. Mandevilla*. Reprinted 1963.

SPANISH EDITIONS. There are five early editions of a Castilian text, whose relationship to the surviving unique manuscript at El Escorial is unclear. Each edition contains 120 woodcuts, with occasional additions, and after the *editio princeps* is basically a resetting of its immediate predecessor. Copies of editions of 1515 and 1564 are reported but not known to be extant.

1521 Jorge Costilla. Valencia. [BL C 20 3. 32]
1524 Jorge Costilla. Valencia. Reprinted Madrid 1958. [Biblioteca Nacionale, Madrid R 13149]
1531 Jorge Costilla. Valencia. [Hispanic Society of New York, 107 M 31]
1540 Juan Navarro. Valencia. [BL 567 i. 5]
1547 Alcalá de Henares. [BL 149 e. 6]
1952 J.O. Marsh, 'The Spanish Version of *Mandeville's Travels*', an edition of the 1521 print, collated with the 1540 print. U. of Wisconsin Ph. D. 1952
1958 *Libro de las Maravillas del Mundo*, intro. E.M. Ferrando. Madrid. A reprint of the 1524 edition. A limited edition of 250 copies.

1980 P.L. Montañes, *Libro de las Maravillas del Mundo. Saragossa.* An edition of
     the El Escorial manuscript.

DANISH EDITIONS. There are no early editions.

1857 C.J. Brandt, *Gammeldansk Laesbog* I. 115–23 prints extracts. Copenhagen.
1881-2 M. Lorensen, *Mandevilles Rejse in gammeldansk.* 3 vols. Copenhagen.

DUTCH EDITIONS. There are two incunable editions, five 16c. editions (all printed
at Antwerp: *c.* 1530, 1550, 1564, 1578, 1592), six 17c. editions (all printed at
Amsterdam except the fifth: *c.* 1610, *c.* 1630, *c.* 1650, 1656, 1677 Antwerp, 1697),
and nine 18c. editions.

[*c.* 1470] printer and city unknown [BL C 2 m. 5]
1494 Govaerdt Back. Antwerp. [BL G 6707]
1908 N.A. Cramer, *De Reis van Jan van Mandeville.* Leiden.
1918 S. Martinnsson, *Mandeville's Reisebeschreibung in Mittelniederdeutscher
     Übersetzung.* Lund.

SECONDARY SOURCES

A.R. Bart, 'La "Langue Romanesque" del *Voyage d'Outremer* di Jean de Mandeville', *Aevum* 58 (1984) 287–300.

I. Bejczy, 'De wereldkaart van John de Mandeville', *Millennium* 3 (1989) 99–105.

J.W. Bennett, 'The Woodcut Illustrations in the English Editions of Mandeville's Travels', *Papers of the Bibl. Soc. of America* 47 (1953) 1–11.

— 'Chaucer and *Mandeville's Travels*', *MLN* 68 (1953) 531–4.

— *The Rediscovery of Sir John Mandeville*, PMLA Monograph XIX (1954).

A. Borgnet and S. Bormans, *Ly Myreur des Histors* (1864–87), 7 vols.

A. Bovenschen, 'Untersuchungen über Johann von Mandeville und die Quellen seiner Reisebeschreibung', *Zeitschrift der Gesellschaft für Erdkunde zu Berlin* (1888).

C. Brown, 'The Authorship of the *Pearl*', *PMLA* 19 (1904) 149–53.

C. Burnett and P.G. Dalché, 'Attitudes towards the Mongols... Mandeville', *Viator* 22 (1991) 153–67.

D.R. Butturff, 'Satire in *Mandeville's Travels*', *AnM* 13 (1972) 155–64.

K.W. Cameron, 'A Discovery in John de Mandevilles', *Speculum* 9 (1936) 351–9.

A.C. Cawley, 'A Ripon Fragment of *Mandeville's Travels*', *ES* 28 (1957) 262–5.

— 'Mandeville's Travels: a Possible New Source', *NQ* 217 (1972) 47–8.

V. Chauvin, 'Le prétendu séjour de Mandeville en Egypte', *Wallonia* 10 (1902) 237–42.

H. Cordier, 'Jean de Mandeville', *T'oung pao. Archives de l'Asie orientale* 2 (1891)

L. de Backer, *L'Extrême-Orient au moyen âge* (1877).

J. De Kock, 'Quelques copies aberrantes des *Voyages* de Jean de Mandeville', *Le Moyen Âge* 71 (1965) 521–37.

C. Deluz, *Le Livre de Jehan de Mandeville. Une Geographie au XIVᵉ siécle* (1988).

G. De Poerck, review of Letts 1949, *Revue belge de philologie et d'histoire* 30 (1952) 881–3.

— 'La tradition manuscrite des *Voyages* de Jean de Mandeville', *Romanica Gandensia* 4 (1956) 125–58.

— 'Le corpus mandevillien du ms. Chantilly 699', *Fin du Moyen Age et Renaissance. Mélanges offerts à Robert Guiette* (1961) pp. 31–48.

— 'Le manuscrit Supersaxo 99 de la Bibliothèque cantonale de Valis', *Vallesia* 26 (1971) 97–110.

M. de Riquer, 'Le Voyage de Sir John Mandeville en Català', in *Miscellània d'homenatge a Enric Moren-Rey*, ed. A. Manent i Segiman *et al.* (Abadia de Monserrat, 1988).

M. Doyle and M.C. Seymour, 'The Irish Epitome of *Mandeville's Travels*', *Éigse* 12 (1967) 29–36.

W.J. Entwistle, 'The Spanish Mandevilles', *MLR* 17 (1922) 251–7.

R. Fazy, 'Jehan de Mandeville. Ses voyages et son séjour discuté en Egypte', *Asiatische Studien* 1.4 (1950) 30–54.

F. Fery, 'Un extrait des *Voyages* de Jean de Mandeville: le chapitre du baume', *Romania* 105 (1984) 511–25.

R.H. Fife, *Der Wortschatz der englischen Mandeville nach der Version der Cotton Handschrift* (1902), with corrections by C.G. Osgood in *American Journal of Philology* 28 (1907) 90–4.

W.G. Ganser, *Die niederlandische Version der Reisebeschreibung Johanns von Mandeville* (1985).

W.P. Gerritsen, 'Mandeville en het astrolabium', *De nieuwe taalgids* 76 (1983) 481–95.

T. Gobert, 'Un célèbre voyageur. Mandeville', *Chronique archéologique du pays de Liège* 12 (1923) 3–11.

A. Goosse, review of Letts 1953 and Bennett 1954 in *Les Lettres Romanes* 14 (1960) 80–5.

— 'Les lapidaires attribués à Mandeville', *Les Dialectes belgo-romans* 17 (1960) 62–112.

— 'Jean de Mandeville et Jean d'Outremeuse', *Festschrift Walter von Wartburg* (1968) I. 235–50.

R. Hanna, 'Mandeville', *Middle English Prose. A critical guide* (1984) pp. 121–32.

Z. Haraszti, 'The Travels of Sir John Mandeville', *Boston Public Library Quarterly* 2 (1950) 306–16.

P.J. Horner, '*Mandeville's Travels*. A new manuscript extract', *Manuscripta* 24 (1980) 171–5.

D.R. Howard, 'The world of *Mandeville's Travels*',*Yearbook of English Studies* 1 (1971) 1–17.

— *Writers and Pilgrims. Medieval pilgrimage narratives and their posterity* (1980).

I. Jackson, 'Who was Sir John Mandeville? A fresh clue', *MLR* 23 (1928) 466–8.

H. Lange, 'Chaucer und *Mandeville's Travels*', *Archiv* 174 (1938) 179–81.

— 'Die Paradiesvorstellung in *Mandeville's Travels*', *Englische Studien* 72 (1938) 312–4.

J. Lejeune, 'Jean d'Outremeuse', *Annuaire d'histoire liégeoise* 4 (1951) 457–525.

R. Lejeune, 'Jean de Mandeville et les Liégeois', *Mélanges... offerts à M. Maurice Delbouille* (1964) II. 409–37.

M. Letts, *Sir John Mandeville. The man and his book* (1949).

— 'A fifteenth-century manuscript of Sir John Mandeville's Travels', *Quarterly Bulletin of the South African Library* 3 (1949) 110–2.

— 'The source of the woodcuts in Wynkyn De Worde's edition of *Mandeville's Travels* 1499', *The Library* 3rd. ser. 6 (1951) 154–61.

— 'A German manuscript of *Mandeville's Travels* dated 1433', *MLR* 50 (1955) 57–60.

M.J. Lidman, 'The Travels of Sir John Mandeville. A checklist', *Thoth* 15 (1975) 13–18.

D. May, 'Dating the English translations of *Mandeville's Travels...*', *NQ* 232 (1987) 175–82.

D. Metlitzki, *The Matter of Araby in Medieval England* (1977).

E. Montegut, 'Sir John Mandeville. L'homme et le conteur, le philosophe', *Revue des Deux Mondes* 96 (1889) 277–312, 547–67.

E.J. Morrall, 'Michel Velser and his German translation of Mandeville's *Travels*', *Durham University Journal* 55 (1962) 16–22.

— 'Oswald von Wolkenstein and Mandeville's *Travels*', *Medieval German Studies presented to Frederick Norman* (1965) pp. 262–72.

— 'The text of Michel Velser's 'Mandeville' translation', *Probleme mittelalterlicher Überlieferung und Textkritik*, ed. P.F. Ganz and W. Schröder (1966) pp. 183–96.

C.W.R.D. Moseley, 'The lost play of Mandeville', *The Library* 5th ser. 25 (1970) 46–9.

— 'Sir John Mandeville's visit to the Pope. The implications of an interpolation', *NM* 54 (1970) 77–80.

— 'Chaucer, Sir John Mandeville, and the alliterative revival. A hypothesis concerning relationships', *MP* 72 (1974) 182–4.

— 'The metamorphoses of Sir John Mandeville', *Yearbook of English Studies* 4 (1974) 5–25.

— 'The availability of *Mandeville's Travels* in England', *The Library* 5th ser. 30 (1975) 128–32.

— 'Behaim's Globe and *Mandeville's Travels*', *Imago Mundi* 33 (1981) 89–91.

— *The Travels of Sir John Mandeville* (1993).

F. Mossé, 'Du nouveau sur le Chevalier Jean Mandeville', *Études Anglais* 8 (1955) 321–5.

L. Mourin, 'Les lapidaires attribués à Jean de Mandeville et à Jean à la barbe', *Romanica Gandensia* 4 (1955) 159–71.

J.J. Munro, 'Sir John Mandeville's Egypt', *Egypt and Sudan Diocesan Review* 3 (1924).

D. Murray, *John de Burdaeus or John de Burgundia otherwise Sir John Mandeville and the Pestilence* (1891).

— *The Black Book of Paisley* (1885).

E.B. Nicholson, letters to *The Academy* 11 Nov. 1876, 12 Feb. 1881.

— 'John of Burgundy...', *The Academy* 25 (12 April 1884) 261–2.

— and H. Yule, 'Sir John Mandeville', *Encyclopaedia Britannica*, 9th. edition (1883).

J. Richard, 'Voyages réels et voyages imaginaires', *Culture et travail intellectuel dans l'Occident médiéval*, ed. G. Hasenohr et J. Longère (1981) pp. 211–20.

F.E. Sandbach, 'Otto von Diermeringen's German translation of *Mandeville's Travels*', *MLQ* 2 (1899) 29–35.

— *Handschriftliche Untersuchungen über Otto von Diemeringen deutsche Bearbeitung der Reisesbechreibung Mandeville's* (1899).

L. Schepens, 'Quelques observations sur la tradition manuscrite de *Voyage* de Mandeville', *Scriptorium* 18 (1964) 49–54.

A. Schörner, *Die deutschen Mandeville Versionen* (1927).

M.C. Seymour, 'A medieval redactor at work', *NQ* 206 (1961) 169–71.

— 'The origin of the Egerton Version', *Medium Aevum* 30 (1961) 159–69.

— 'Secundum Johannem Maundvyle', *English Studies in Africa* 4 (1961) 148–58.

— 'The Irish version of *Mandeville's Travels*', *NQ* 208 (1963) 364–6.

— 'The early English editions of *Mandeville's Travels*', *The Library* 5th. series 19 (1964) 202–7.

— 'Mandeville and Marco Polo. A stanzaic fragment', *AUMLA* 21 (1964) 39–52.

— 'The scribal tradition of *Mandeville's Travels:* the Insular Version', *Scriptorium* 18 (1964) 38–48.

— 'The English epitome of *Mandeville's Travels' Anglia* 84 (1966) 27–58.

— 'The English manuscripts of *Mandeville's Travels*', *Trans. Edinburgh Bibl. Soc.* 4 (1966) 169–210.

— 'A fifteenth-century East Anglian scribe', *Medium Aevum* 37 (1968) 166–73.

— 'A letter from Sir John Mandeville', *NQ* 219 (1974) 326–8.

— 'The scribe of Huntington Library MS. HM 114', *Medium Aevum* 43 (1974) 139–43.

— 'Medieval America and Sir John Mandeville', *An English Miscellany Presented to W.S. Mackie*, ed. B.S. Lee (1977) 46–53.

— 'De Worde's 1503 edition of *Mandeville's Travels*', *Bodleian Library Record* 13 (1990) 341–2.

— review of Deluz, *ES* 72 (1991) 568–70; of Metlitzki, *ES* 61 (1980) 556–9; of Morrall, *Medium Aevum* 45 (1976) 329–32; of Zacher, *RES* 39 (1978) 79–81.

— and R.A. Waldron, 'The Danish version of *Mandeville's Travels*', *NQ* 208 (1963) 406–8.

D.W. Singer, 'A note on Sir John Mandeville', *The Library* 3rd. series 9 (1918) 275.

K. Sisam, *Fourteenth-Century Verse and Prose* (1921).

A. Steiner, 'The date of the composition of *Mandeville's Travels*', *Speculum* 9 (1934) 44–7.

E.G.R. Taylor, 'The cosmographical ideas of Mandeville's day', in Letts 1953, I.

J.D. Thomas, 'The date of *Mandeville's Travels*', *MLN* 72 (1957) 165–9.

H.J. van der Meer, *Main facts concerning the syntax of Mandeville's Travels* (1929).

J. Vogels, 'Das Verhältniss der italienischen Version der Reisebeschreibung Mandeville's zur französischen', *Festschrift dem Gymnasium zu Mörs... gewidmet* (1882).

— *Die ungedruckten Lateinischen Versionen Mandeville's* (1886).

— 'Handschriftliche Untersuchungen über die englische Version Mandeville's', *Jahresbericht über das Realgymnasium zu Crefeld* (1890).

C.K. Zacher, *Curiosity and Pilgrimage. The literature of discovery in fourteenth-century England* (1976).

F. Zarncke, 'Die Reisebeschreibung des Johannes von Mandeville', *Abhandlungen der philologische-historische Classe der königlische sächsische Gesellschaft der Wissenschaften* 8 (Leipzig, 1883) 128–53.